You Are Respectfully Invited
to Attend My Execution

You Are Respectfully Invited to Attend My Execution

Untold Stories of Men Legally Executed in Wyoming Territory

Larry K. Brown

HIGH PLAINS PRESS

FIRST PRINTING

10   9   8   7   6   5   4   3   2   1

*The cover art, based on historic photographs, is by B.J. Durr.
Cover art © B.J. Durr*

Library of Congress Cataloging-in-Publication Data

Brown, Larry K.
You are respectfully invited to attend my execution : untold stories of
men legally executed in Wyoming Territory / Larry K. Brown.
p.   cm.
Includes bibliographical references and index
ISBN 0-931271-42-8 (hard)
ISBN 0-931271-41-X (soft)
1. Criminals--Wyoming--Biography.
2. Capital punishment--Wyoming--History--19th century.
I. Title.
HV6785.B76   1997   97-2511
364.6'6'0922787--dc21   CIP

HIGH PLAINS PRESS
539 CASSA ROAD
GLENDO, WYOMING 82213

DEDICATION

Florence, Ronan, Maura, Evan and Courtney

The wretch who has defied her [the law's] most sacred commands, and has thought to creep through ways where she was not, finds that his path ends with her, and beholds beneath her hood the inexorable face of death...

OLIVER WENDELL HOLMES
CHIEF JUSTICE, U.S. SUPREME COURT

CONTENTS

In this fascinating collection of stories, Larry Brown tells about the lives and the deaths of some of territorial Wyoming's most notorious badmen. He has combed the archives, newspaper sources, and court records to compile these accounts of how law and order, at least occasionally, functioned in territorial Wyoming.

As the stories reveal, some of the men who were executed might have been innocent. The frightening fact about capital punishment, then and now, is that the law is not infallible. Many were assuredly guilty or, as former Tom Horn defense counsel and later federal judge T. Blake Kennedy once observed about his famous client, he might have been wrongfully convicted of murdering a young boy he didn't kill, but he certainly had killed others.

Perhaps most interesting about these stories, laced with pathos, depravity, and unspeakable violence, is the fact that Wyomingites did not resort to mob violence in these cases. Whether it was for deterrence, retribution, or punishment, the executions described on these pages from the "wild west frontier" of territorial Wyoming were carried out only after the legal process was followed. To some readers, this may come as a surprise. Each of these men had his "day in court." This belies the notion that Wyoming Territory was "lawless" or that the only justice came from the end of a gun.

The author distinguishes from the outset between lynchings and executions. Yet, as these stories demonstrate, in a territory where the population barely surpassed 60,000 in 1890, capital punishment was effectuated with some frequency.

These stories tell us that in a lightly populated frontier territory, law was in place. Murderers were convicted, sentenced,
and executed. Wyomingites, by and large, respected the rule
of law and supported those in whose hands it was placed even
with all its frailties. Only through such cooperation could
they build together a civilized and just society. These
accounts, so ably told by Larry Brown, give us a glimpse of
how it was done.

PHIL ROBERTS, J.D., PH.D.
DEPARTMENT OF HISTORY
UNIVERSITY OF WYOMING

The events that led me to this book were almost as serendipitous as the circumstances from which these historical accounts evolved.

From childhood, I heard the most exciting stories from my family about Captain Emmet Crawford, a paternal great-uncle, who earned his spurs during the Civil War and later in the great Indian Wars of the West with the U.S. Army's Third Cavalry. Crawford served at such outposts on the high plains as Fort D.A. Russell near Cheyenne, Wyoming, Forts Robinson and Sidney in Nebraska, and at various military encampments in northern Colorado and Nevada. He also accompanied Brigadier General George Crook's Bighorn and Yellowstone Expedition of 1875–76 during which he fought at historic battles on the Rosebud and at Slim Buttes in the Dakota Territory. He and his comrades subsequently survived the "Starvation March" into the Dakota Territory by eating their pack mules and horses. Later while he was assigned to the Army in the Southwest, a marauding band of irregular Mexican troops killed Crawford as he led an expedition into Mexico to capture Geronimo, the notorious Apache leader. Coincidentally, Crawford's chief scout on that campaign was Tom Horn, who was later convicted of murdering a boy near Iron Mountain. Authorities executed Horn by hanging him in Cheyenne on November 20, 1903.

But of all the exciting tales I heard at my relatives' knees, one of the most intriguing concerned Crawford's capture of renegade WILLIAM "TOUSANT" KENSLER.

When I "retired" in 1992 to indulge my passion for historical research and writing, the Kensler story came to mind and soon dominated my study of available documents at the Wyoming State Archives in Cheyenne. There, I discovered the rest of the story. In a fit of jealous rage over a "soiled dove," Kensler shot and killed one of his lover's many suitors at the infamous Six Mile "hog ranch" near old Fort Laramie. He was hanged in Cheyenne on November 19, 1874—the second person legally executed in the Wyoming Territory.

So who was the first? Additional research unveiled JOHN BOYER, another regular patron of the Six Mile, who shot two men there after a dance. He paid for that crime at the end of a rope on April 21, 1871, also in Cheyenne.

Before July 10, 1890, when Wyoming became our nation's forty-fourth state, an additional five men stretched the string for committing the ultimate crime: murder in the first degree.

JOHN LEROY DONOVAN, alias "John Lee" or "Jack Lee," was executed in Rawlins on January 18, 1884, for bludgeoning and robbing a Rock Springs barber.

The fourth murderer, GEORGE COOKE, shot his brother-in-law, an East Side Elementary School custodian in Laramie City on Thanksgiving Day in 1883. Cooke was hanged for that crime thirteen unlucky months later in the same city.

JOHN OWENS, known best as "William" or "Bill" Booth, beat to death an old German settler in Johnson County. After being convicted, Owens with his head in a noose met his Maker in Buffalo, Wyoming, on March 5, 1886.

BENJAMIN F. CARTER bullied a young cowboy during a roundup in the northwestern part of Carbon County before shooting him in their tent. The law hanged the "Badman from Bitter Creek" on October 6, 1888, in Rawlins for that offense.

And, lastly, vindictive GEORGE A. BLACK put three fatal bullets into the body of a litigious hermit as the old man sat cutting seed potatoes in his cabin. Then, with the help of accomplice Dwight Rockwell, he torched the body within the shadow of Pole Mountain in Albany County.

These stories could not have been told well, however, without the extraordinary help of the Wyoming State Archives staff. Senior historians Cindy Brown, Curtis Greubel, and Carl Hallberg were particularly helpful with their professional guidance and suggestions.

Paula West Chavoya, who prior to retirement supervised the Wyoming State Museum's Photographic Research Section, and her assistant LaVaughn Bresnahan also are enthusiastically commended. Their vast knowledge of Wyoming history plus their ability to anticipate and provide the photography needed to illustrate its principal characters, places, and events continue to impress me.

Credit, too, must go to artist Eileen Hayes Skibo of Wellington, Colorado, whose unique sketches from nearly indiscernible newspaper art salvaged five of the only known likenesses of this book's protagonists.

And I am indebted to Mark Junge, former editor of *Annals*, the Wyoming State Historical Society's membership magazine, for his friendship and encouragement as well as his extraordinary insight and perspective regarding Wyoming history.

Phil Roberts, a professor at the University of Wyoming Department of History, has my heartfelt thanks, too, for his constructive guidance. Dr. Roberts's superior knowledge of

Wyoming history, plus his experience and expertise as a lawyer and author, provide an intelligent, insightful foreword that is as entertaining as it is instructive.

I also would be remiss if I did not recognize Nancy Curtis of High Plains Press whose professional criticism and support made this publication possible.

Lastly, I am most grateful to my best friend, my love, my greatest booster, my most uncompromising critic, and my spouse. Thanks to Florence—my writing matures and becomes more polished by her fine eye, sense of humor, and love of language.

LARRY K. BROWN
CHEYENNE, WYOMING, 1997

What is the purpose of this book? Certainly, it is not to explain the science or philosophy of law. Neither is it to excuse nor analyze the twisted minds of the seven star-crossed men who during Wyoming's territorial days (July 25, 1868–July 10, 1890) snuffed the lives of eight victims. Simply stated, I found so compelling the circumstances that *legally* put each felon's neck in a noose that I preserved their stories for posterity.

You may notice that I distinguish between legal punishment for a crime, as opposed to lynching or some other form of mob reprisal against a suspected criminal. Lynching, as defined during the heavy-handed Jacksonian era of "President Andy" (1832-1845), was the "extra-legal infliction of punishment or exercise of correctional power which resulted in personal injury." For example, when some believed that Wyoming authorities failed to adequately enforce the laws between 1882 and 1903, vigilantes meted out their own justice by "stringing up" an estimated thirty-three men and one woman for a variety of real and imagined crimes. Conversely, from Wyoming's territorial days until statehood twenty-two years later, only seven individuals were formally tried for crimes by juries of their peers, convicted, and executed according to laws passed by their duly elected representatives.

A BRIEF HISTORY OF CAPITAL PUNISHMENT

The death penalty has an ancient history as evidenced by the executions of Socrates and Jesus. The impression that past generations favored or regularly practiced such retribution, however, seems to be mistaken. In fact, the death penalty fell into disuse during the time of the Roman Republic and, as evidenced in Thucydides's book *The Peloponnesian War*, was heatedly challenged for many of the same reasons voiced today.

Ironically, the use of capital punishment in the Western World gained increased acceptance with the rise of Christianity during the Middle Ages, apparently because the clergy emphasized the individual's responsibility for his own behavior. And, for those incapable of controlling themselves, the church had no qualms about using force to reform and salvage the sinners. According to Sir Francis Palgrave, a leading nineteenth-century British historian, poet, and morality spokesman, discipline should be "imposed for the good of the offender; in order to afford the means of amendment, and to lead the transgressor to repentance and to mercy."

But, with the passage of time, the punishment pendulum swung from those theologically directed forms of discipline back toward the even more severe means of revenge offered by the state. And it was during the transitional period—from the Norman Conquest in 1066 to the restoration of Charles II in 1660—that the English parliamentarians refined their laws by defining what constitutes a crime:

1) a conscious, voluntary external harm must be demonstrated; 2) the act must have been legally prohibited at the time it was committed; 3) the offender must have possessed criminal intent (mens rea) when he participated in the crime; 4) there must be a fatal causal relationship between the voluntary misconduct and the legally

forbidden result; and 5) there must be some legally pre-
scribed punishment for the person convicted of the crime.

Many of the offenses described are the same we suffer
today: murder, manslaughter, larceny, robbery, burglary,
arson, rape, and mayhem.

So effective were those definitions and the penalties to
be imposed that they became part of the legal traditions
brought by emigrants to the New World, even though there
seemed to be little uniformity in the way they were applied
throughout the colonies. Hanging, for example, was
imposed not only for murder, but also for many lesser
crimes, including pick-pocketing and petty theft. Further,
there was no distinction of degree regarding heinous crimes,
although cause could reduce the charge of "murder" to a
lesser offense, such as "manslaughter." Despite some evidence of growing sophistication and humanity as practiced
by the colonists, punishment could be as severe and cruel as
any experienced in the past. Take, for example, the following 1780 sentence by a Delaware Court:

...that you be hanged by the neck not till you be dead,
for you must be cut down alive. Then your bowels must
be taken out, and burnt in your face, then your head
must be severed from your body, and your body divided
into four quarters, and these must be at the disposal of
the Supreme Authority of the State.

After the American Revolution, the number of offenses
punishable by death declined. Then, with the passage of the
Pennsylvania Statute of 1794, as influenced by the Declaration of Independence and the Constitution of the United
States, murder for the first time was divided by degrees of

During a two-day spree, a vigilance committee lynched "Big Steve" Young and three other men in Laramie to rid their town of self-appointed city officials. When Young refused their orders to "git out of town," the vigilantes dragged him to the foot of B Street, near the rail-road tracks, and hanged him from a telegraph pole. Like a giant sun-dial, his shadow marks the execution hour at 10 A.M. (Courtesy of Wyoming Division of Cultural Resources)

severity with capital punishment authorized only for first-degree murder. Although other states and territories, including Wyoming, soon adopted similar legislation, many variations continued to exist. In fact, many were so complex that, lacking general knowledge and sufficient education, most Americans either knew little about or failed to comprehend their rights. Worse, even their lawyers sometimes lacked an understanding of the statutes, even if they had access to them. Law books and libraries, too, were scarce on the frontier, a matter bemoaned by the editor of the

Wyoming Weekly Leader when the first Wyoming Territorial Legislature convened in 1869:

> *One of the first subjects which should receive the attention of the Legislature is that of founding a Territorial Library* [that should] *comprise three principal departments: the literacy, or library proper; the law library, and the Historical Museum.... The second department should comprise the "law library," embracing all the best general and special works on jurisprudence with extensive collections of State reports...the administration of justice would thus be greatly facilitated.*

Even years later, members of the New Mexico Territorial Legislature are said to have written to the U.S. Congress claiming they were:

> *...unable to obtain a copy of the statutes, even for their own use.... In 1880, neither the governor, the legislature, the chief justice, the United Stated attorney, nor any Territorial official, except the secretary, was in possession of the law they were expected to be guided by and to administer.*

Considering such circumstances, it is even less likely that lesser officials owned complete sets. In fact, most officers of the lower courts—justices of the peace, sheriffs, coroners, clerks—were so poorly informed and trained about their duties that they were forced to depend upon privately-printed, simply-worded manuals for most of their instructions.

THE PURPOSE OF PUNISHMENT

Criminal law was created to prevent socially undesirable conduct by punishing violators. The reason frequently put forth for such action is revenge — to get even. A second theory is that if the convicted criminal is made to suffer his misery may deter others from doing the same. Thirdly, and especially true in the case of capital punishment, is that once the death penalty is carried out against the guilty, it is an indisputable fact he never again will commit crime.

Regardless of which reason one may accept, the simple fact is that the majority believes it is the right and, indeed, the duty of a state to write and apply law. Regrettably, "hanging judges" and vigilantes also have used that rationale to justify their actions.

METHODS OF CAPITAL PUNISHMENT

One of the main reasons criminals were put to death in pre-industrial times was that the public had few practical choices for dealing with the guilty. Imprisonment, particularly long-term lock-up, required money and resources that a poor or developing society, like that in the American West, was either unable or unwilling to spend. So, in the absence of other acceptable solutions, killing offenders became one of the most widely practiced forms of criminal punishment.

An astonishing variety of methods to produce death has been used throughout the centuries. The favored modes of execution in England, for example, were burning and beheading, sometimes accompanied by such refinements as drawing and quartering the victim's body. Hanging later became the preferred penalty. It was the custom, too, that the prisoner be given the opportunity, en route to his public execution, to stop at a local tavern for a "parting cup." Additional trappings for such events included the sale of box seats to spectators, encouraging the theater of public confessions by the condemned, and the marketing of pamphlets depicting the sordid crime for which the felon was to be punished. Some argue that such spectacle served as a deterrent to potential offenders and probably prevented some secret executions of the innocent. Still others point out that such counter-productive carnivals only aroused morbid curiosity.

Although modern hanging techniques almost always ensure the victim's neck will be broken immediately, it was not always so. Ex-hangman Albert Pierrepoint once explained that during most of the eighteenth and nineteenth centuries, legal hanging was really death by slow strangulation. As terrible as that may have been, at least one witness argued that the anticipation of being strangled was worse than the act itself. Wyoming's Second District Court Judge M.C. Saufley recalled that as a Confederate officer during the Civil War, he had been captured by Union troops. After being selected to be hanged, he was forced by his captors to stand in the shadow of the gallows, daily expecting to be executed. Only fear of retaliation by the enemy, he said, caused the Union soldiers to cancel their plans. Later, as an officer of the court, Saufley ordered death by hanging, adding with assurance that he "probably knew more about it [the act of hanging] than anyone else in the area." As a lad, he said, an overly playful, older youth once lassoed and choked him into unconsciousness. According to Judge Saufley, the sensation he experienced was "not only entirely painless, but rather pleasurable and interesting."

Hanging, which was the prescribed method of executing a condemned prisoner in Wyoming's territorial days, included a variety of carefully orchestrated procedures: constructing the gallows of precise dimensions; selecting a rope of sea grass or hemp; properly tying the "hangman's knot;" lubricating the slip noose with soap, candle wax, or grease; positioning the knot at the base of the left ear to quickly and fatally break the spine near the base of the neck; binding securely the victim's limbs; offering the prisoner an opportunity to offer his last words; providing a "spiritual advisor" to offer religious counsel prior to execution; and medically assuring the victim's death before burial. Although law did not direct such details, most were applied in each case because of historical precedent as well as man's inherent need for ritual.

CAPITAL PUNISHMENT IN THE WYOMING TERRITORY

When the first Legislative Assembly of the newly formed Wyoming Territory convened in Cheyenne on October 12, 1869, one of the first issues regarding law was introduced before the Legislative Summary Council by Representative William S. Rockwell (D-Carter County), chairman of the Judiciary Committee. He called for "an Act adopting the common law of England and certain declaratory and remedied states of said Kingdom," transplanting our English forefathers' framework of laws to the high plains of America. Before that same Legislature adjourned, it built a legal base for the handling of criminal trial and punishment based on the principles found in one of our nation's most treasured documents, the Declaration of Independence, which states that:

> *...all men are created equal; that they are endowed by their Creator with certain inalienable rights; that among*

these are life, liberty and the pursuit of happiness. That
to secure these rights, governments are instituted among
men, deriving their just powers from the consent of the
governed....

It affirms, too:

...in the name and by the authority of the good people of
these [the original thirteen] *colonies, solemnly publish*
and declare...that, as free and independent states, they
have full power to levy war, conclude peace, contract
alliances, establish commerce, and to do all other acts
and things which independent states may of right do.

This, of course, included the creation and enforcement
of laws they believed were necessary to protect the life and
liberties guaranteed by the Constitution.

The people's Council and House of Representatives also
drew upon the wisdom of the founding fathers who, in their
preamble to the U.S. Constitution, made clear:

We, the People of the United States, in Order to form
a more perfect Union, establish Justice, insure domestic
Tranquility, provide for the common defense, promote
the general Welfare, and secure the Blessing of Liberty to
ourselves and our posterity....

To protect such rights, the framers of our Constitution
included Article II, Sections I and II to assign the power for
administering laws to authorities of a clearly defined system
of courts. Specifically:

The judicial power of the United States shall be vested in
one supreme court, and in such inferior courts as the
congress may, from time to time, ordain and establish.

Section II elaborates:

(1) The judicial power shall extend to all cases, in law and equity, arising under this constitution, the laws of the United States... between citizens and a state.... (2) In all the other cases before mentioned, the supreme court shall have appellate jurisdiction, both as to law and fact, with such exceptions, and under such regulations, as the congress shall make. (3) The trial of law crimes...shall be by jury; and such trial shall be held in the state where the said crimes shall have been committed.

Despite the unprecedented protection of the U.S. Constitution, Americans remained guarded and concerned about their rights. To enhance their protection from perceived as well as real abuse, they directed their representatives to add Article V which states:

No person shall be held to answer for a capital or otherwise infamous crime, unless on a presentment or indictment of a grand jury...nor shall [any person] be compelled, in any criminal case, to be witness against himself, or shall be deprived of life, liberty or property, without due process of law.

They also insisted on the inclusion of Article VI:

In all criminal prosecutions, the accused shall enjoy a right to a speedy and public trial by an impartial jury of the State and district wherein the crime shall have been committed, which district shall have been previously ascertained by law, and to be informed of the nature and cause of the accusation; to be confronted with the witnesses against him; to have compulsory process for obtaining witnesses in his favor; and to have the assistance of counsel for his defense.

As further protection of individual rights, Article VIII was added to insure "Excessive bail shall not be required, or excessive fines imposed, nor cruel and unusual punishments inflicted."

Thus, with the approval of the U.S. Congress on July 25, 1868, of a "Temporary Government for the Territory of Wyoming," the power to enforce the aforementioned rights was delegated to the Territory's judicial system. And from that power came procedures deemed necessary to establish categories of crime, as well as to prescribe appropriate punishment for each type. The death of a person, for example, "perpetrated by means of poison, or lying in wait, or by another kind of wilful, deliberate and premeditated killing, shall be deemed murder in the first degree, [the perpetrator upon conviction] shall suffer death by hanging by the neck." So specific, in fact, were the criminal procedures that they even described where and how such punishment were to be carried out:

SECTION *170: When any person shall be sentenced to be hung, such punishment shall be inflicted in the immediate vicinity of the jail, within an enclosure... higher than the gallows, and so constructed as to exclude the view of persons outside thereof.*

SECTION *171: Execution Within Jail: In all cases in which the jail in any county shall be of any construction that the sentence of death can be conveniently carried into execution within its walls, no enclosure need be prepared, as is provided in the preceding section, but such execution shall take place within the walls of the jail.*

SECTION *172: No Jail In County: Whenever the sentence of death shall be about to be carried into execution in any county of this territory which at the time has no jail, it shall be the duty of the sheriff to cause such execution to be conducted at such convenient place at the county seat as he may select.*

SECTION *173: Who May be Present: Besides the sheriff and his assistants, the following persons may be present at the execution, and none others: The clergyman in attendance upon the prisoner, such other persons as the prisoner may designate, not exceeding six in number, and such other persons as the sheriff may designate, not exceeding twelve in number.*

SECTION *174: Whenever the sheriff shall deem the presence of a military force necessary to carry into effect the provisions of the four preceding sections, he shall make a written requisition upon the officer of the militia highest in command then in his county, who shall issue the necessary orders to insure a compliance with the requisition of such sheriff.*

SECTION *175: Whenever the sheriff shall inflict the punishment of death upon a convict, in obedience to the command of the court, he shall make return of his proceedings as soon as may be, to the clerk of the court where the conviction was had, and the clerk shall subjoin the return to the record of conviction and sentence by recording the same.*

SECTION *176: If any convict sentenced to the punishment of death, shall appear to be insane, the sheriff shall forthwith give notice thereof to a judge of the district court of the judicial district, and shall summon a jury of twelve impartial men to inquire into such insanity; at a time and place to be fixed by the judge, and shall give immediate notice to the prosecuting attorney.*

SECTION *210: If any person who has been convicted of murder in the first degree, and sentenced to be hung, shall escape, and shall not be retaken before the time fixed for his execution, it shall be lawful for the sheriff to re-arrest such person, and commit him to the jail of the proper county, and make return thereto to the court in which the sentence was passed, and there upon the court shall proceed to fix the time of execution, which shall be carried into effect by the proper officer, as may be provided by law for the execution of persons convicted of murder in the first degree.*

THE FIRST LEGAL EXECUTION
IN THE WYOMING TERRITORY

The laws adopted and formed in creating the Territory's own Constitution apparently served the people well in trying the vengeful John Boyer. Following his conviction of murder in the first degree, the young man of French-Indian blood became the first person executed in accordance with the Territory's new criminal codes when authorities hanged him in Cheyenne on April 21, 1871. Certainly Governor Campbell seemed satisfied with his administration's handling of that first capital punishment case. In his biennial message to the Joint Session of Council and House of Representatives, he said this about "Enforcement of Laws:"

It is a matter of pride and congratulations that in our new territory the tone of society is such that crime meets with no toleration whatever, and the laws are so faithfully enforced by the courts that there is no longer any excuse for the formation of vigilance committees, as was the case previously to the organization of the territory. Although these self-constituted committees for the enforcement of order and the punishment of crime had been common, there has not been a single instance of unlawful punishment of crime since our territorial organization was affected.

As circumstances changed, laws were added and amended to correct and refine weaknesses. Such adjustments were made necessary, in part, because of experience gained through the prosecution and conviction of additional criminals. Two cases that contributed to such changes included John Leroy Donovan's May 6, 1883, bludgeoning to death of a Rock Springs barber and George Cooke's drunken shooting of his brother-in-law in Laramie some six-and-a-half months later. Such criminality was responsible, at least in part, for motivating the Territorial Representatives to differentiate between felonies—crimes that may be punished by death or imprisonment—and those other criminal offenses deemed "misdemeanors." This they did with an addendum entitled an "Act Declaring the Criminal Law Governing This [Wyoming] Territory."

Despite the politicians' claims of good law enforcement and legislative initiatives for improving criminal law and procedures, the courts failed for a variety of reasons to convict many murder suspects. That inability to assure justice, in turn, caused public resentment and editorial complaints. In fact, claimed a *Laramie Times* reporter in a March 1882 article, although there had been "scores of murders, cold-blooded and atrocious" within the past fifteen years, most had gone unpunished. In the rival *Sentinel* newspaper the following month, editor Dr. James H. Hayford also decried the violence: "It has actually come to be regarded as less danger to kill a man than to steal a horse."

It would be two years later, however, before the Legislative Assembly convened under the leadership of Governor William Hale to further refine the Compiled Laws of Wyoming. Specifically, Justice Code, Title II, Offenses Against the Person of Individuals (Chapter 35, Section 15) was amended to insure that death resulting from the act of rape, arson, robbery or burglary would be designated murder in the first degree. Amendments also included those to Chapter 39, which dealt with criminal intent:

In any indictment for murder in the first degree, or murder in the second degree, or manslaughter, it shall not be necessary to set forth the manner in which or the means by which the death was caused, but it shall be sufficient to charge in any indictment for murder in the first degree that the defendant did wilfully, deliberately and of his malice aforethought, premeditatedly kill and murder the deceased.

Given the timing of that amendment, it is reasonable to assume its passage was influenced by the publicity and public's furor stemming from the high drama of Donovan's trial as well as the Territorial Supreme Court's subsequent denial of his attorney's plea for a new trial. Only weeks later, John Owens butchered an old German gentleman in a cabin on Dry Creek.

By the time the Legislative Assembly convened in January 1888, not only had Owens "swung" for his crime, but badman Ben Carter had suffered the same fate for putting a bullet in the brain of a fellow cowboy during a roundup. Under the administration of Governor Thomas Moonlight, the lessons learned from such cases are believed to have influenced the March 9, 1888, approval of the following changes to the Revised Statutes of Wyoming (Section 1879):

The coroner shall hold an inquest upon the dead bodies of such persons only as are supposed to have died by unlawful means, or the cause of whose death is unknown. When the coroner is notified that the dead body of any person, supposed to have died by unlawful means, or the cause of whose death is unknown, has been found within the limits of his county, it shall be his duty to summon forthwith six citizens of the county to appear before him at the time and place named to act as jurors at the inquests, who shall receive two dollars each day and ten cents per mile for each mile actually and necessarily traveled while engaged upon said inquest. The coroner shall also, when necessary, furnish means of transportation for the jury and witnesses to and from the place of inquest and for the removal of the body, and for any necessary expenses actually incurred, as provided in this section, and for the subsistence of the coroner, jurors and witnesses and for forage for animals, the claimants shall present their accounts in duplicate, attested by the coroner or acting coroner, as the case may be to the board of the county commissioners of the county, and if found correct and just the same shall be paid in warrants, properly drawn, upon the order of the country commissioners.

Several months before the last Territorial (Eleventh) Legislative Assembly met in Cheyenne in January 1890, George Black shot a Pole Mountain hermit to death in adjoining Albany County. For that crime, Black suffered the people's wrath a month later and gained dubious distinction as the last man to be executed before Wyoming became a state.

Now that you know a bit about the history of capital punishment and how it came to Wyoming, I would like for you to meet your hosts. Remember? They invited you to attend their executions.

John Boyer

"Look at Me!...I Die Brave!"

On October 27, 1870, John Boyer claimed his place among history's footnotes when he fired a lead slug from his seven-dollar revolver into William H. Lowry's left breast. A split second later, he sent a round into the gut of James McClusky, a well-known U.S. Army interpreter at Fort Laramie. Those rash acts put Boyer on a path that, despite a brief detour, sent him up the gallows steps to become the first person legally executed in the Wyoming Territory.

The trouble started one night earlier that month when the namesake son of French trapper-trader and gold prospector John Boyer [Jean Baptiste Bouyer] returned home and found his widowed Yankton Sioux mother and sister bound and gagged. He believed Lowry and McClusky, who spent much of their time at Fort Laramie, also raped the women.

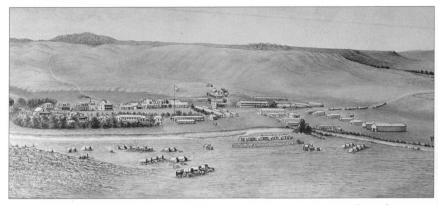

Fort Laramie was not much larger or more prosperous when this sketch was made in 1889 than when John Boyer revenged the rape of his mother and sister by murdering William H. Lowry and James McClusky, October 1870, at the nearby Six Mile hog ranch. Less than two years later—April 1872—William "Tousant" Kensler also committed homicide at the infamous "ranch" for which he too was tried and convicted before dying of "hemp fever." (Courtesy Wyoming Division of Cultural Resources)

Several nights later, on October 30, Boyer discovered the two brutes at the Six Mile hog ranch, an infamous brothel, saloon and gambling den about six miles southwest of Fort Laramie on the Baptiste Fork of the Sybille River. After turning in his weapon to the bartender for safekeeping, Boyer entered the dance hall, where he found his foes.

Waiting until about 2 A.M., Boyer retrieved his pistol from the barkeep and left the building. A short time later, he mounted his horse and rode back to the door where he called McClusky and Lowry out of the building, threatening to whip them for what they did to his family. As the two men appeared at the door, the twenty-six-year-old avenger pulled his revolver and, without warning, shot and killed them both. Boyer immediately fled undeterred and hid with a local band of Sioux. The Indians, fearing reprisals, turned him over to the authorities who were demanding his release. Colonel F. F. Flint, commander of the Fourth Infantry at Fort Laramie, wired his headquarters in Omaha, Nebraska: "All [the Indians] are behaving well; the Sioux delivered up the murderer of McCloskey [*sic*] and say they want to do right. I sent him to Cheyenne to be delivered to U.S. Marshal."

On December 13, Sheriff T. Jeff Carr transferred Boyer to Fort D. A. Russell, near Cheyenne, and locked him in the overcrowded and poorly ventilated guardhouse there until the First District Court of Laramie County convened on March 21, 1871. According to a local newspaper account, the courtroom was "...graced by the presence of a large number of ladies of Cheyenne, anxious to witness personally, the workings of judicial proceedings." Much of their interest in this trial undoubtedly stemmed from the fact that, for the first time in that city's history, members of their sex served as jurors. This dramatic development came only fourteen months after Wyoming's Territorial Legislature granted women in the state the right to vote.

Despite the strong evidence against him, Boyer chose to plead not guilty only to have the jury members rule unanimously on March 23 to convict him of murder.

WALK AWAY ESCAPE

A week later, Boyer threatened to foil the noose when he escaped about noon from his cell by simply walking past the guard and out into the nearby prairie. Condemning the lapse of security, an irate reporter observed, "Being properly ironed, and guarded by sentinels, his escape seems very strange. It is sheer nonsense to suppose that he could escape if the sentinels were doing their duty." Although a commander sent his company of cavalry in pursuit, the soldiers returned without the escapee. Exactly how Boyer escaped went undisclosed, but some speculated, "He was doubtless aided in getting away by several half-breeds, who are said to have been hanging around the quarters for a few days past."

Regardless of the reason for his ability to take "french leave," his captors claimed a $300 reward several days later when they arrested him en route to his home near Fort Laramie. "He was met on the road walking alone, and with his handcuffs off and fastened to his belt," according to witnesses. "Seeing the coach coming, he left the road, and while the stage was passing a curve in the road, hiding him from view, he secreted himself under the bank of a ravine, and was only discovered and recognized as the stage had passed his place of concealment." Fort Laramie officials quickly sent Captain Robert P. Wilson and a detachment of Company A, Fifth Cavalry, armed and ready, to the area where witnesses had last seen the murderer. Fortunately, Boyer did not refuse the "invitation" of Captain Wilson's superior force for an escorted trip back to Cheyenne.

The "half-famished" felon, having had no food for four days for fear of being recognized by ranchers in the area, partook with eagerness of the lunch which was offered by the soldiers. With Boyer's feet badly frozen and very painful,

Sheriff T. Jeff Carr, Laramie County's famed lawman, had the dubious distinction of tripping the traps beneath the feet of the first two men legally hanged in the Wyoming Territory: John Boyer and William "Tousant" Kensler. (Courtesy Wyoming Division of Cultural Resources)

authorities put him on the next stage, under guard, to Cheyenne, where he arrived on Sunday evening, April 2.

RETURNED TO JAIL

Back in jail, Boyer amused himself during the long, lonely hours by sketching. Impressed with the prisoner's artistic skill, a local reporter, who saw the drawings, wrote:

[He] *made a very creditable portrait of himself suspended from the gallows, the court room, the judge who pronounced the sentence, and the jury which found him guilty of murder. In his picture he gives the lady members of the jury a horrid appearance. Boyer either has no eye for womanly beauty, or else he is opposed to women's rights.*

Finally, on April 10, U.S. Marshall John Slaughter and Deputy John O'Brien let newsmen into the jail where they kept Boyer and four other prisoners. Heavily ironed in a very small, dark cell Boyer responded to media questions about his escape by saying he only escaped so he could return to Fort Laramie to see his mother and sister. If successful, he added, he planned to return to Cheyenne for his punishment "without a murmur," because he regretted being drunk and killing McClusky and Lowry. The reporters, impressed with his intelligence, sensitivity, and contrite demeanor, reported as much in their news copy.

Only five days before his execution, Boyer suffered a "severe attack of cholera morbus" that local newsmen speculated might help him cheat the gallows. The following day, after learning of his improved condition, those same reporters again turned their attentions to drumming up local interest and readership. They even started a daily

Accused murderer John Boyer sketched the Laramie County Courtroom while he awaited the verdict of the first Cheyenne jury in which women participated. "In his picture he gives the lady members of the jury a horrid appearance," one newsman reported. "Boyer either has no eye for womanly beauty, or else he is opposed to women's rights." Boyer also claimed he got the first hint of his fate when he heard jurors say, regardless of the evidence, they would "hang the d--d half-breed." (Courtesy Wyoming Division of Cultural Resources)

countdown toward his execution with such one-liners on the local news page as "Four more days for Boyer." Another filler item reported that Sheriff Carr, who returned to Cheyenne after delivering some prisoners to Detroit, stopped in Chicago where he purchased rope plus some other "necessary articles for the execution of Boyer."

On the eve of Boyer's demise, anticipation in Cheyenne built to such a level that even the newspaper people questioned the circus atmosphere they helped create. They also tried discouraging the anticipated heavy public turnout by

United States Marshal John Slaughter took custody of John Boyer after his brief escape from the Fort D. A. Russell guardhouse near Cheyenne. Slaughter subsequently oversaw Boyer's final hours at the Laramie County jail and escorted him up the gallows to the noose. (Courtesy Wyoming Division of Cultural Resources)

writing that the hanging would not be done in public. "This information," according to the press, "will serve to put at rest that species of morbid and depraved curiosity which impels some persons to a desire to witness a hanging." That admonition, however, came only after the reporters interviewed Boyer in his cell and secured their own ringside seats at the hanging.

THE EXECUTION

Finally, before noon on April 21, local law enforcement authorities led Boyer from his cell, out of the jail, and across the street to a secluded grout building on Sixteenth Street.

Long before the fateful hour, a large crowd gathered outside the building and, at times, became very noisy and boisterous. Many skeptics anticipated a last minute reprieve for Boyer. Others guessed, with no justification, that Boyer's friends might try to rescue him at the last moment. In the streets near the building, special officers had difficulty restraining the excited crowd that pushed in windows and doors in their eagerness to witness the event. During that confusion, D.C. Tracy of Pine Bluffs, in his zeal to get a peek at the prisoner, scuffled with special policemen A. Gavin and Henry Canfield. When Tracy refused Gavin's order to "stand back or be arrested," Canfield drew his revolver and slapped a gash in Tracy's head.

In the meantime, as the clock ticked, authorities ushered supervising physicians G.W. Carey and G.H. Russell inside the old building to witness the grisly ceremony. Reverend J.D. Davis, pastor of the Congregational Church in Cheyenne, who doubled as Boyer's "spiritual adviser," accompanied the two doctors. A few Territorial and city officers, newsmen, and "leading citizens, who had been made special deputies" also entered the makeshift execution chamber.

At 12:30 P.M., the sheriff and his men led their prisoner up the scaffold steps. Dressed neatly in a clean white shirt, Boyer "bore a pleasant expression upon his face," according to witnesses. With his arms tied firmly behind him, he sat quiet and composed in a chair as the sheriff read the death sentence. Asked if he had anything to say, Boyer replied, "Look at me! I no cry; I no woman; I man. I die brave!" Without further delay, Reverend Davis delivered the obligatory prayer as the sheriff placed a noose around Boyer's neck and pulled a black hood over his face. A moment later, the young man dropped through the trap door and into the cellar. Only his struggling head and shoulders were visible above the floor. Three minutes later, the sheriff's assistants removed the body and placed the remains in a plain wooden coffin to be buried "in accordance with the desire of the prisoner" in the old city cemetery at the north end of Bent Street.

"Thus endeth the first legal execution which ever took place in Wyoming," proclaimed the local newspaper. "Let it be a warning to others who have not yet learned that the laws must be obeyed and criminals punished."

Unfortunately, history soon forgot that lesson. The justice system saw six more men legally hanged in the Wyoming Territory before "Cowboy Country" attained statehood on July 10, 1890.

Red Cloud, the great chief of the Oglala Sioux, sent shivers of terror down the spines of Cheyenne residents when he professed "great friendship" for the condemned John Boyer. They feared the chief, who participated in the Fetterman Massacre, might help the convicted murderer escape execution. (Courtesy Wyoming Division of Cultural Resources)

Sources Cited

The primary source documents used in developing this chapter are contained in Territory of Wyoming vs. John Boyer, Laramie County, First Judicial, District Court Criminal Case Files #1-114 and #1-189, 1871, on file at the Wyoming State Archives in Cheyenne. Included in these records are Boyer's Indictment as well as his Execution Order.

For detailed background about young Boyer's family, John Gray's outstanding book, *Custer's Last Campaign: Mitch Boyer and the Little Bighorn Reconstructed* (Lincoln, Nebraska: University of Nebraska Press, 1993) proved most useful. Mitch, half-brother of John, gained fame as a celebrated frontiersman and military scout, who died with General Custer in their final battle with Indians near the Little Bighorn River in Montana. Elnora Frye's *Atlas of Wyoming Outlaws at the Territorial Penitentiary* (Laramie, Wyoming: Jelm Mountain Publications, 1990) also is an imperative reference for anyone seriously interested in Boyer or any other convict who served time in the Wyoming Territorial Penitentiary.

Of the many personal recollections concerning old Wyoming, Emma Cross Morton's Collection (#9849-91-11-04) at the American Heritage Center at the University of Wyoming in Laramie offered many details about several of the characters in this chapter. It also provided numerous anecdotes not found elsewhere. Although the total collection includes six large boxes of George Harry Cross's unpublished recollections and memorabilia, the main source of information pertaining to this chapter may be found in *Braehead Memories*, Vol. I, 1853-1883, Chapter "Labonte Creek Ranche, Subsection: Fort Fetterman-1876."

Lastly, official accounts available in the Post Returns, Medical Histories and Letters Received (1868-1874) concerning Fort Laramie and Fort D.A. Russell enhanced descriptions of the military's pursuit and capture of Boyer. I culled additional details concerning this case from "Thomas Jefferson Carr: A Frontier Sheriff," as published in the Wyoming State Historical Society's *Annals of Wyoming* (Vol. 20, No. 2, July, 1948), as well as from those issues of the *Cheyenne Daily Evening Leader* covering the period of the events. All of the information referred to in this paragraph is available at the Historical Research and Publications Section of the Wyoming Department of Commerce in Cheyenne.

William "Tousant" Kensler

Hunter Turns Killer
at the Six Mile Hog Ranch

SAD BUT TRUE. The "half-breed" hunter and the Mexican hired hand courted the same hog ranch honey. She encouraged their visits and sought their attention. They, in turn, bought her charms. Why not? Those vices may have been sins, but they certainly weren't crimes. Besides, the men's money put bread and beans in her belly during those tough times. She just hoped the two lovers did not come to call at the same time, but it happened one evening in April 1872.

The hunter, William "Tousant" Kensler, all too frequently left his seventeen-year-old wife Mary and their two children at their Fort Laramie home to ride southwest to visit the infamous Six Mile hog ranch on Sybille Creek. There, the twenty-three-year-old Romeo liked to tip a brew and pay for a poke with the girls who worked there.

During one of his many trips to the ranch, he met Jennie Hogan to whom he often returned. Little is known of this young woman except that, at twenty-two years of age, she probably had seen more of the seamy side of life than her youth deserved. Also, she had at least one other regular customer: Adolph Peña, a local sheepherder.

It is believed Kensler first came to the ranch to enjoy a night of fuss and feathers, but soon became a regular customer there. As the son of a German father and Sioux Indian mother, he apparently felt quite at home at the Six Mile operated by Jules Ecoffey with the help of his friend Adolph Cuny. They shared a cultural bond as the owners' wives were Indians.

Hog Ranches:
A Phenomenon of the Old West

Hog ranches, a phenomenon of the Old West, found favor near military camps and forts where troops guarded rail and stage lines. These establishments offered space where a man could while away his leisure time with a shot of rye, a game of faro, and a roll in the crib with a "soiled angel," made passably attractive by loneliness and miles of sage. And habitués claimed one of the worst in the west was the infamous Six Mile ranch. "Bud" Thomason shot its original owner, John Hunter—the first man known to be killed there in October 1868. Two years later, John Boyer planted Lowry and McClusky during their visit to that spa. At least one more man, Perry Harbour, a wood chopper, bit the dust at the Six Mile when George W. Blake shot him on August 13, 1871.

Despite its rowdy reputation—or perhaps because of it—the ranch attracted off-duty soldiers from nearby Fort Laramie. It also seemed to pull trash from the trail, including nearly every grifter, gambler, bandit, hustler, and whore passing through that area.

THE CRIME

So, on April 9, 1872, the Six Mile added still another sordid chapter. The evening may have started quietly enough as customers drifted into and out of the bar. Suddenly, Kensler and Peña found themselves in the same room—at the same time—with their lover. As words turned personal and grew more heated with each drink, Peña "sneeringly taunted" Kensler about his relationship with Jennie. Kensler's rage and retorts proved equally provocative.

Suddenly, Peña broke from the room and headed upstairs where he slapped on his revolver. Through the dim, flickering light cast by oil lamps that hung from the rough-hewn beams, Kensler saw Peña returning with iron on his hip. Sensing danger, he quickly left the bar. Angry and embarrassed at being skedaddled, he pulled a $20 Winchester carbine from the scabbard on his saddle and returned to the building. Standing outside, Kensler fired a slug through a window and into Peña's left side, where it pierced Peña's spleen, stomach, and liver before coming to rest under the skin on the far side of his body.

THE ESCAPE

Although it is not clear as to the exact chain of events, Justice of the Peace E.E. McCammon responded to the local

The Three Mile hog ranch served as "Tousant" Kensler's brief haven after he fled another, nearby, saloon-brothel where he murdered his love rival. Three Mile "soiled doves" once entertained customers in the "cribs" or one-room apartments of this building constructed of grout. Grout, an early form of cement, consisting of coarse gravel instead of sand. (Courtesy Wyoming Division of Cultural Resources)

citizens' call for official help. He, in turn, contacted Fort Laramie military authorities. Captain Guido Ilges of the Fourteenth U.S. Infantry immediately issued an order, on behalf of his commander, directing Captain Elijah R. Wells to assemble a pursuit detachment and run Kensler to ground. With the help of famed military scout Baptiste "Big Bat" Pourier, Captain Wells summoned a non-commissioned officer with six privates of Troop E, Second Cavalry, and the small force promptly mounted their horses and left to arrest Kensler. In the meantime, the murderer raced through the night towards another, equally notorious, hog ranch.

The Three Mile, also owned by Cuny and Ecoffey, sat among low hills about three miles southwest of Fort Laramie. Kensler, tired and his horse winded, reached the ranch at sunrise the next morning. T.H. Hopkins, who claimed he lived there, testified later that Kensler "said he had killed a Mexican on the Sabille [sic]. His horse looked as if he had been hard ridden." Hopkins surmised Kensler and his horse covered about thirty to forty miles before arriving at his home.

After a brief rest, the felon fled again as Hopkins raced to Fort Laramie to tell officials of Kensler's confession. At about 9 A.M., Kensler showed up again, this time at Joseph [José] Armijo's spread about six miles from Fort Laramie, where the killer "stopped but a few moments, [and] said that he had killed a man."

THE CAPTURE

Whether confused, distraught, or simply in need of a drink, Kensler returned to the Three Mile ranch. There, Captain Wells and his men found Kensler, but when the fugitive saw the troops, he vaulted into his saddle and again tried to escape. After running his horse for about a mile, Kensler surrendered to the soldiers' restraints after his mount gave out. When asked why he shot Peña, Kensler said simply: "Jealousy." He later added that "Peña went up stairs and came down with his revolver on. I went out...saddled my horse...went to the window...and there Peña was shot."

Taken under guard to Fort Laramie, Officer of the Day Lieutenant T.B. Briggs put his captive in "close confinement under guard until further orders" in the military guardhouse. The structure, used until 1876, sometimes accommodated about two dozen prisoners in an unheated and unlighted sub-story room. Furniture and bedding consisted only of those items that prisoners brought with them. The garrison mess provided the prisoners' food.

THE WHEELS OF JUSTICE TURN

Peña "languishing did live" until April 10. Post Surgeon Dr. Edward J. O'Callahan, who conducted the post-mortem two days later, reported, "In my opinion surgical aid would have been of no avail, as the hemorrhage which was the cause of death could not be arrested." In the meantime, acting Coroner and Justice of the Peace McCammon held an inquest on April 12 to determine Kensler's role in the crime. The verdict: Guilty!

Authorities subsequently moved Kensler eighty miles south to Fort D.A. Russell near Cheyenne, where they locked him in the guardhouse before transferring him to the Laramie County jail at the corner of Nineteenth and Ferguson [now Carey] in downtown Cheyenne. The First Judicial District officials in Laramie County took court actions shortly thereafter.

Kensler's attorney, William H. Miller, wasted no time and spared no effort in trying to extricate his client from his predicament. Despite Miller's deft legal maneuvers, however, nothing swayed the judicial authorities to support his pleas. Consequently, on December 9, after a jury found Kensler of "sound memory" and having "feloniously" shown "malice aforethought," presiding judge E.A. Thomas declared him guilty of "Murder in the First Degree." He further directed that Kensler be:

The guardhouse at Fort Laramie held "Tousant" Kensler before he was transferred to Cheyenne where he was tried and executed for murdering a sheepherder. The structure held about two dozen prisoners in an unheated and unlighted sub-story room. There was no furniture. Bedding consisted only of the blankets which prisoners brought with them. (Courtesy Wyoming Division of Cultural Resources)

> ...taken hence to the prison whence you came to be there kept in the custody of the Sheriff of Laramie County, until the day of execution or—and that on Thursday, the 2d Day of January A.D. 1873,—within the walls of the prison of said county or within an enclosure to be provided for the purpose in accordance with the requirements of the laws of the territory—between the hours of 12 o'clock A.M. and 2 o'clock P.M. Of said day you be there and there hanged by the neck until you are dead.

The far right tip of diamond shaped Fort D.A. Russell is the guard-house, where authorities imprisoned John Boyer and Tousant Kensler before they became the first two men legally hanged in Wyoming. Their crimes? Boyd bid two fellow Six Mile ranch customers farewell with a seven-dollar revolver while Kensler killed a rival for the favors of a hog ranch bawd. (Courtesy Wyoming Division of Cultural Resource)

Still trying to avoid the inevitable, Kensler's lawyer obtained a stay of execution by filing the first ever appeal to the Wyoming Supreme Court to stay all proceedings until the case could be reviewed and, hopefully, overturned. When the justices upheld the lower court's sentence, the court rescheduled Kensler's hanging to November the following year.

ESCAPE FROM LARAMIE COUNTY JAIL

While awaiting the court's decision on his appeal, Kensler and cell mate horse thief John Barnes broke out of the unguarded Laramie County jail on Monday evening, July 7,

1873. Laramie County's Sheriff Carr started in pursuit the next morning, but when he learned about the loss of two fine horses belonging to Durbin Brothers, he terminated the chase. "It is likely," he said, "that the jail birds appropriated the horses to aid them in making good their escape."

Reporters, who examined the jail from which the criminals escaped, found that Barnes removed one of the metal rods from the iron grating surrounding the cells. Although Sheriff Carr had reported several months earlier that the rod was damaged, members of the Laramie County Grand Jury responsible for its repair did nothing. Exploiting that failure to act, Barnes used the iron bar to break off the padlock of Kensler's cell and they crawled through that opening in the grating and into the hall. After removing the padlock from the outer door that led into an area surrounded by a ten-foot high brick wall, they simply crawled over the barrier. "Without saying a word to any one, they bid adieu to the hospitable people of Laramie county" and found their way to freedom.

INDIAN CAMP HIDEOUT NEAR RED CLOUD AGENCY

From Cheyenne, Kensler escaped to the Red Cloud Agency near Fort Robinson in Nebraska. Being part Sioux, he hid with Little Wound's Oglala Sioux band, in which he easily blended with his Indian friends. He even painted his face and wore tribal clothing to make it harder for the lawmen to find him. Despite his disguise, Kensler's vile temper soon became a lightning rod for more trouble. Upon meeting his old nemesis Captain Wells near the Agency, he "told him he would shoot him or any other man who would attempt to capture him."

In an effort to accelerate Kensler's capture and return him to Laramie County, the Wyoming Territory's Governor John Allen Campbell wrote to the Honorable Columbus Delano, U.S. Secretary of the Interior. He informed him that Kensler and Barnes "had escaped from custody and made their way across the Platte River where they are safe from pursuit under the terms of the Treaty of 1868 having effectively closed the country north of the Platte from the Whites." Requesting the Secretary's help, he asked

> ...that the Agent of the Sioux Indians at the Red Cloud Agency [J.J. Saville] be directed to demand of the Sioux the presentation of the escapees. They could be delivered either to the Agent or the Military authorities at Fort Laramie and the Sheriff of Laramie County...where he would take them into custody.

The Governor added with apparent confidence that such action "will teach criminals that the Indian country is no longer an asylum for them."

LIEUTENANTS CRAWFORD AND RAY
CAPTURE THE "HALF-BREED"

On Sunday, June 13, 1874, Lieutenant Emmet Crawford, Third Cavalry, and Lieutenant P.H. [Patrick Henry] Ray, Eighth Infantry, drove from their camp in an ambulance to the Red Cloud Agency. There they learned Kensler had left the trader's store and gone to the rear of the stockade overlooking the Niobrara River. Several other off-duty soldiers also happened to be at the store.

Crawford reveled in his good fortune at finding the felon. As his Third Cavalry friend Lieutenant Charles Morton recalled, Crawford told him that "it made his blood boil to think of that renegade defying the authority of the state and the nation and he made up his mind to capture him." Lieutenants Ray and Crawford borrowed a Winchester rifle from the trader and cautioned him to be on the lookout. Then, with their fellow troopers, they went in search of the outlaw for whom a large reward had been offered. Turning the corner of the blockhouse, they found Kensler seated at the edge of the river bank, talking to a Indian woman. Before they could take action, however, Kensler jumped over the edge of the bank. The two officers, splitting one to the left and the other to the right, rushed forward to where they found Kensler trying to cross the stream on a log. Ray quickly shot him through both legs. Crawford, with the other men, pulled Kensler out of the water while Ray called for their ambulance. They brought their prisoner up the bank and lay him on the floor of the wagon. Then, as Ray sat in the back with his rifle to stop anyone who tried to approach, the driver lashed the mules to run for Fort Robinson. "The Indians got their ponies and arms as quickly as possible and there was an exciting race for camp," according to Morton, but Crawford and Ray brought in their man.

The action against Kensler so incensed the Indians that the officers experienced some tense moments before they got their prisoner safely to Camp Robinson. Had Chief Red Cloud and some of his fellow chiefs not interceded by helping to keep the other Indians at bay, it is unlikely that Crawford and Ray would have succeeded in returning Kensler to the post.

Shortly after the two soldiers and their captive arrived at the camp, the sudden, noisy rush of Indian pony herds near

Captain Emmet Crawford, Third Cavalry, Company G, helped cap-
ture the murderous "Tousant" Kensler at the Red Cloud Agency in
Nebraska Territory after the killer escaped from Fort D.A. Russell's
guardhouse near Cheyenne. Mexican irregular troops shot Crawford's
brains out—literally—in 1886 as he led a U.S. military expedition
into Mexico in pursuit of Geronimo. (Courtesy Captain Crawford's
niece, Mrs. Ruth O. (nee Brown) Dunn; Fort Collins, CO)

its perimeter startled those inside. Native boys, tending the horses, had been signalled by elders with flashing mirrors to return to their village. The Indians quickly dismantled their tepees, apparently preparing to leave the area. Fearing the warriors might rush the camp in an attempt to rescue Kensler, who had been put in double irons in the hospital tent, the soldiers immediately went on alert. Nothing happened, however, until about midnight when the Indians began firing from behind Lieutenant W.H. Carter's tent. According to the lieutenant:

We had all lain down with our arms prepared for such an emergency. Upon leaving my tent the Commanding Officer called to me in the dark to take command of the first company, which was without officer. As I started towards it with pistol in hand, I suddenly found myself astride a man crawling on the grass, and, as I was admittedly very much shocked, I cocked my pistol when I recognized the voice of our Irish soldier cook, who said "Don't shoot—it's Finnerity." I don't know which of us was most scared, but I was always prompt to admit that I did not like being astride an Indian in the dark. Finnerity had put his belt on upside down, running to join his company, and spilled his cartridges in the grass, and had turned to pick them up when I encountered him.

While Lieutenant Carter untangled himself, the other soldiers formed a skirmish line and moved towards the Indians' flashing guns. The Sioux fell back in the face of the soldiers' gunfire before the troops withdrew to their camp where a large portion of the command kept guard the rest of the night. "I lay down," continued Carter, "but before daylight I was summoned by the corral master, who informed me that while the firing was proceeding a party of Indians had come in between the cavalry and infantry and torn down the corral fence, and had driven off our entire supply of beef on the hoof." Lieutenant Crawford and the cavalry troop immediately went in pursuit and recovered a large number of the stolen cattle along the White River.

On June 21 Crawford, with six privates from his Company G, escorted Kensler via train to Cheyenne. A week later, the lieutenant and his men arrived in Cheyenne, the "Magic City of the Plains," where they turned over the murderous Kensler to Sheriff Carr.

NEWSMEN VISIT KENSLER IN CHEYENNE JAIL

Because of his past foul deeds and infamous exit from the Laramie County jail, reporters soon flocked to interview Kensler in his cell at Cheyenne's calaboose. Why had he killed Peña, they wanted to know. He said, he:

...committed the act from the combined effects of whiskey, drunk during the evening, of the threats said to have been made by the deceased [whom he called a Mexican "Greaser"] *and from the jealousy and rage occasioned by the presence of the deceased who sneeringly taunted him in the presence of the girl whom they both were in love with— "courting."*

In reply to their questions about his trial, Kensler complained to reporters that:

He knew he could not expect an unprejudiced trial, being not a white man, and gave as evidence of it, the declarations that he heard made in the court room during the time of his trial, when citizens said they would "hang the d—d half-breed any how." He charged that if he could have procured the attendance of parties whom, he said, he asked should be summoned, and the services of a fair interpreter, that he could have shown that his crime was not murder.

He also claimed witness John Boyd had:

…purposely suppressed the circumstances of threats and gestures made by the deceased, and the meeting with the girl, who embracing him [Kensler] begged him to stay and not leave her alone with that man, which circumstances, in his partially intoxicated condition, so aroused his evil passions that in a moment of anger and jealously he fired the shot. He added that he had no idea a moment before of doing the deed. And says he could prove it if allowed an opportunity.

That said, Kensler ended the interview by asking for a priest.

"As we were about to leave," reported the newsmen, "we offered to lend him any aid we might be able to render, in making known his wishes and wants to his friends and people. As we bade him 'good-bye' and promised to publish his story and wishes, at the mention of his 'two little childs,' the Father's love mastered the man, and we left him bowed down among his fellow convicts."

With time running out, Kensler's Indian friends sent a petition on November 3 through Indian Agent Saville to President Ulysses S. Grant asking that Kensler be pardoned. "Messrs. Red Cloud, Spotted Tail, Man-Afraid-of-His-Horses, Red Dog, Grass, Blue Nose and a number of other sub-chiefs

The Laramie County jail, circa 1873. The small, brick annex imme-diately behind and to the right of the three-story Laramie County Courthouse was home to John Boyer and Tousant Kensler until they hanged for murdering men at a "hog ranch" near Fort Laramie. The courthouse was located at what is now the northwest corner of Nineteenth Street and Carey Avenue. (Courtesy Wyoming Division of Cultural Resources)

and warriors of the two Sioux bands living north of this city [Cheyenne]" signed the request for clemency.

CROWDS TRY TO SEE CONDEMNED MAN IN CELL

On the day before Kensler's execution, many stockmen and ranchers from the Fort Laramie area rushed to Cheyenne to see him swing from the gallows. In a last ditch effort, attorney Miller sent a plea to Governor Campbell asking for either a pardon or the commutation of his client's sentence. Kensler, despite those pressures, however, failed to lose sleep over his predicament. He simply went to bed at 9 P.M. that evening and "enjoyed a deep, unbroken slumber."

The next morning (November 19, 1874) "dawned beautifully" as a crowd gathered at the jail, asking questions about the prisoner's attitude and condition. Some clung to the barred window near his cell in the hope they might get a peek at the "Six Mile killer," but only a few satisfied their curiosity. Awaking at 7 A.M., Kensler had his last breakfast from Sheriff Carr's private table. A short time later, Catholic priest Father McGoldrick went to the prisoner's cell, where "Kensler showed a warm religious feeling." According to the priest, the prisoner "did not manifest any fear to meet his impending doom, but on the contrary, exhibited coolness, free from bravado."

HE DIED WITH HIS SHOES ON

At 12:15 P.M., Kensler, accompanied by Sheriff Dayton of Albany County, Father McGoldrick, and Sheriff Carr with his assistants, entered the old stone McDonald Building at the corner of Bent and Twenty-first streets. For years, many knew that site as Tracy's Corral. There, near the gallows, waited a few select spectators with cards of admittance. Kensler and the priest took seats near a warming fire, where they whispered together before ending their chat with a silent prayer.

At Sheriff Carr's signal, Deputy W. Taylor unceremoniously led the prisoner to the platform. Kensler, without showing the least hesitation or tremor, climbed the stairs to the waiting noose. He took his seat upon a chair that had been placed there for him and, with his eyes fixed upon the sheriff's face, listened intently as the death warrant was read. When

Sheriff Carr asked if he had anything to say, Kensler replied, "I have nothing to say, only to ask permission not to die with my shoes on." Apparently his request was ignored. Father McGoldrick immediately moved towards the platform. In a voice quivering with emotion, the priest offered a brief prayer that Kensler repeated word-for-word: "Jesus died for me; Jesus, I love thee." The condemned man said nothing more before the priest bid him farewell with, "God bless you." Quickly, the sheriff adjusted the rope and knot with care so the fall would break Kensler's neck as painlessly as possible. Then, as the priest moved his hand in the sign of the cross over Kensler's head, the sheriff stepped behind the condemned man and tied his hands behind his back before draping a loose, black hood over his head. The sudden darkness caused Kensler to tremble so that the sheriff called for an assistant to steady the prisoner. Father McGoldrick, too, stepped forward and assured Kensler, "Have confidence in your God and He will have mercy upon you."

At 12:28 P.M., Sheriff Carr sprung the trap door and Kensler dropped about five feet into the cellar. No great struggle followed as witnesses saw only a slight tremor in the body. Although the last spark of life seemed extinguished eight minutes later, the attending physicians did not pronounce him dead until 12:50 P.M. Soon thereafter, authorities cut down Kensler's body and placed it in a coffin. When no family or friends claimed the remains, the county authorities buried Kensler that afternoon with a public ceremony.

SOURCES CITED

The primary source documents—Indictment, subpoenas, witness testimony, etc.—used in developing this chapter may be found in the Territory of Wyoming vs. Kinsler [*sic*], Laramie County, First Judicial District Court Criminal Case File #2-85. These records, like most comparable Wyoming criminal case materials, are on file at the Wyoming State Archives. Additional valuable research documents regarding this case, include the Inquest Proceedings, Testimony and Post-mortem Report concerning Adolph Peña, as well as Governor John A. Campbell's Letterpress Book, also are located at the Archives.

For background regarding the time and conditions in which the crime took place, you will find the following authors and their works particularly helpful: Frye's aforementioned *Atlas of Wyoming Outlaws*, Virginia Cole Trenholm's *Footprints on the Frontier* (Douglas, Wyoming: Douglas Enterprise, 1945) and Agnes Wright Spring's *The Cheyenne and Black Hills Stage Routes* (Glendale, California: Arthur H. Clarke Co., 1949). Although not a primary reference for this particular story, Evans S. Connell's book *Son of Morning Star* (New York, New York: Harper and Rowe, 1984) provides interesting information about Kensler's early exploits in the Black Hills. C.G. Coutant's "Thomas Jefferson Carr: Frontier Sheriff" (Vol. 20, No. 2) and "History of Wyoming" (Vol. 13, No. 4) published in the *Annals of Wyoming* also were helpful references.

Major General William Harding Carter's unpublished and undated "Sketch of Ft. Robinson, Nebraska," which is available at the Wyoming Historical Research and Publications Section, also will be of significance for those interested in the site where Lieutenants Crawford and Ray captured Kensler. Additional details, too, came from Fort Laramie's Post Returns, Medical Histories, and Special Orders. Those documents as well as *Cheyenne Daily Leader* newspaper accounts of that period are available on microfilm at the Historical Research and Publications Section.

Lastly, the *Wyoming Almanac,* a secondary source for the introduction, tipped me as to Kensler's first-ever murder verdict appeal to the Wyoming Supreme Court. This publication is a "must" for anyone interested in the many little known, but interesting facts about Wyoming's history.

John Leroy Donovan

His Landlady's Hammer

THE FIRST COOL, GREY light of dawn peeked through the window and into the bedroom where Bill Leighton, the barber, slept.

Whether he dozed or simply felt restless that May 6 in 1883 can only be surmised. What seems clear is that the flare and acrid smoke of a match probably roused him from bed. Apparently satisfied, he laid down again to try for a few more minutes of sleep before Sunday morning customers arrived at the front door of his adjoining barbershop.

Suddenly the head of a hammer arced through the thin light. Thunk!! Thunk!! Thunk!!

- - - - - -

"Guilty of murder in the first degree!" declared Judge Samuel C. Parks as his gavel ended the trial and cleared the court. That decision put John Leroy Donovan on a sure path toward the gallows.

Donovan, alias "Jack" or "John Lee," had arrived several months earlier in Rock Springs, where he worked briefly for the Blair brothers.

Although strong and able, the young man failed to earn enough money to support the lifestyle he wished to lead. He soon learned, however, that William Leighton, a warm and sociable man, had plenty. Leighton came to Rock Springs about 1879. Despite his Anglo-European surname, those who knew the forty year-old barber believed him to be Brazilian.

"I Killed the S.O.B."

But Donovan, who frequented the barbershop, planned to improve his lot by simply relieving Leighton of his poke. What could be easier? At 10 o'clock that fateful Saturday night, young Donovan slipped through the front door of the dark, unattended barber shop and slipped into the connecting bedroom, where he crawled under the bed to await the barber's return. In a subsequent confession that he later denied, Donovan said:

I waited there until [Leighton returned and] *I thought the barber must be asleep. I moved to the foot of the bed and struck a match. This must have disturbed him for he rose up in bed, got out a minute or two and then laid down again. I waited a long time when I struck another match. This time Leighton turned over in the bed and I had to crawl back again. I then made up my mind to wait until he was fast asleep and it was daylight before I dared to come out. He was sound asleep.*

Authorities executed John Leroy Donovan, alias "John" or "Jack Lee" in Rawlins, Wyoming, on January 18, 1884, for bludgeoning and robbing a forty-year old Rock Springs barber by the name of Bill Leighton. The viciousness of Donovan's crime belied an intelligence and sensitivity later revealed in a note he wrote during his final hours to a woman who befriended him in jail. (Sketch by Eileen Hayes Skibo)

Then in the most vicious, graphic and unrepentant terms, Donovan described what happened next:

I killed the son of a bitch...by striking him three blows on the head with a hammer. The first blow I struck him on the [right] *cheek. When I raised the hammer to strike him, I felt my arm weaken and knew that the blow would not be sufficient to kill him.*

As soon as he was struck, Leighton raised his hand to his cheek and cried out, "Oh, my God! My head!"

I knew that I must strike him hard. I struck him [on the right temple] *with such force that it sunk the head of the hammer in his skin up to the wood in the handle. After I struck him this blow he made a peculiar snorting noise that frightened me terribly. I knew there were people in the next building and the board partition was very thin. I was afraid that they would hear the noise and I struck him another blow over the left eye. He continued to make an unnatural noise when I threw the bedding over his head and stamped him.*

A deathly stillness followed. Putting the hammer —which he had taken from the house where he boarded with Mrs. Margaret Hunter and her son George—on a little table, Donovan took a key from his victim's pants, unlocked the dresser drawer, and quickly pocketed the money he found there:

I then looked out of the window and saw it was almost sun-up. I thought I would crawl under the bed again and stay there until night.

I got under the bed, but was not satisfied to stay there. I looked out of the window again and seeing nobody around I concluded to take the chances of getting out [of] *town.*

He eased through the front door, locking it behind him before walking quietly toward the back of the building. He planned to throw away the key until he remembered the missing hammer.

I concluded to keep it [the key] *until night time and go back and get the hammer. I went down the rear of the buildings and out on the plain four or five hundred yards until I reached the dry creek. I then passed under the culvert and came up on the railroad tracks. I walked back on the track coming into town on the main street. I went into Bill Musgrove's saloon, where I washed myself. From there I went to the meat market and bought some lettuce, radishes and strawberries which* [I] *took to Mrs. Hunter's. After breakfast I went out for my washing at the home of Mrs. Baxter.*

A Boy Discovers the Body

About 11 A.M., several customers stopped by Bill's barbershop for a shave but found the door locked. When no one answered, they became quickly concerned because they knew Leighton had heart disease.

Finding a window unlocked, they helped a small boy crawl into the building. He no sooner entered the back room of the shop than he rushed back yelling, "Somebody...killed the barber."

Dr. E.D. Woodruff immediately rushed to the scene, where he and bystanders forced open the door. One glance left no doubt that Leighton lay brutally murdered with bed clothes tightly packed around his head and shoulders. When they removed the quilts, they found the once familiar face covered with blood and disfigured by three terrible wounds. The bloody carpenter's hammer that lay only five feet away on a stand near the door obviously had caused the damage.

At roughly the same time as Donovan picked up his freshly washed clothes from his laundress, an excited little girl rushed into the room. "The barber has been killed," she cried. Donovan watched through the window as a large crowd, gathering at the nearby shop, began dragging some poor drunk through the streets with blood on his face. "I thought they were going to lynch him and felt like going out and helping him," Donovan said later, "but I remembered having the key of the shop in my pocket and went around the house and threw it in the vault."

A telegram quickly summoned Justice of the Peace Joseph W. Stillman from Green River, some fifteen miles to the west, the county seat located on the river of the same name. Stillman empaneled an inquest jury to examine the evidence. After quickly but carefully evaluating the grisly circumstances they found on-scene, it took the small group of jurors little time to deliberate before their foreman J.M. Tisdel declared that "some person or persons unknown murdered the barber."

DONOVAN IS ARRESTED AS SUSPECT

Soon thereafter local lawmen narrowed their ring of suspects to young Donovan. They learned, for example, that he did not sleep at his boarding house on the night in question, and witnesses saw him early the next morning in Musgrove's saloon "taking a careful wash." Their suspect, who had no money prior to the murder, "was flush immediately after, having some $50 or $60 in his possession." The clincher came when, learning of the evidence, Donovan's landlady asked the court to return her missing hammer.

By now the only unanswered question seemed to be, "Would Donovan make it to trial?" Only the good actions of Mr. Tisdel, the superintendent of the nearby coal mines, persuaded his employees not to swing the prisoner from one of the few trees that had roots strong enough to tap the moonscape soil of that area.

At the preliminary examination, Donovan denied any knowledge of the murder but said that he saw Leighton playing cards with a "stranger" at Musgrove's the night of the murder. The bartender there, unfortunately for Donovan, denied that testimony. Unable to give a more reasonable account of his whereabouts during the night and early morning hours prior to Leighton's death, Donovan found himself being turned over to law enforcement officials in Green River. They, in turn, jailed him there in Sweetwater County's seat of government, to await the grand jury that met five months later.

A RAILROAD DETECTIVE INVESTIGATES

In the meantime, Tisdel wrote to the officers of the Union Pacific Railroad in Omaha, Nebraska, describing the circumstances as he knew them and urging them to send one of their best detectives to help solve the crime. Thomas. L. Kimball, the railroad's assistant manager, responded by sending A.T. Valentine, one of his best sleuths, to make a full investigation.

Arriving at Rock Springs on May 15, 1883, Valentine met with Tisdel to learn the facts. He spent the next day making surreptitious inquiries while trying unsuccessfully to find some clues that might help him untangle the case. Perhaps the best approach, he decided, was to wangle a meeting with the prisoner and gain his trust as well as any evidence that might link him to the crime.

While Donovan remained in the jail, detective Valentine devised a scheme that he hoped would unravel the puzzle. Going to Green River, Valentine met with Sheriff G.L. Vickery. He told the sheriff that he planned to assume the identity of an escaped murderer and asked to be put into Donovan's cell. It took little to persuade the sheriff to help him because the lawmen wanted to share any fame that might come from cracking this case.

On entering the jail, Valentine saw only two prisoners: a Chinese burglar and Donovan. Both convicts curiously eyed their new cell mate. Within half an hour, the sheriff returned to the cell block, where he read aloud a description of the new "prisoner" whom authorities in LaPorte, Indiana, wanted for murder. Just before leaving, the sheriff stared at Valentine's hand. "Give me that ring on your finger; it is described here in this paper as one of the articles stole," said the officer. After taking the ring, Vickery left the jail.

Finding themselves alone, Donovan asked Valentine about his crime. The detective told him that he had killed an old man for his money. The details he shared mirrored those of Donovan's crime. Valentine later told authorities:

> *When I finished my story, I said to Lee* [Donovan] *that a man was a fool to give himself away. He appeared disposed to tell me what he had done, but I did not want*

*him to tell me until I had gained his complete confi-
dence, believing that he would then be more disposed to
make a truthful confession.*

PLANS TO ESCAPE

Throughout the day, Valentine bragged to his cell mates
about his nefarious past, especially murders in which he
claimed to have been involved. He even suggested a plan for
escaping the jail and asked Donovan if he had friends who
might furnish them with the tools they would need. Valentine later recalled:

> *I told him that I was sure that if I could get the right
> kind of a case knife I could make a saw that would
> enable us to get out. He thought a woman of the town
> whom he knew would bring a knife to him, and said he
> would ask the sheriff to ask her to call and see him. He
> suggested that a young man who had been working
> about the jail for his board might be induced to assist us
> in making our escape. He also took into his confidence
> the Chinaman, who agreed to write to his cousin at
> Rock Springs for the kind of knife desired.*

But neither the woman nor the cousin came to the rescue.
Devising another plan, they asked a young man who
worked in the jail to help them escape, and Valentine paid
him $25 to get the knife he said he needed. About an hour
later, the youth returned with the blade. The prisoners
planned to escape five days later by taking Sheriff Vickery's
mounts and riding fifteen miles downriver. Their young
accomplice promised to meet them there with fresh horses
so they could race for the Mexican border. Stalling for time,
Valentine rejected the knife as being the wrong kind and

asked the boy to get him another type. The young man left and, for reasons unknown, never returned. The Chinese prisoner subsequently scuttled their escape scheme by drawing the plan on the wall of his cell "to which he called the attention of the sheriff by means of signs."

Although Valentine's plot failed to break them out of jail, his feigned enthusiasm for the task apparently won Donovan's confidence. The detective remembered that Donovan:

> ...was inclined to be very communicative, and related to me most of his past life. He told me how, on one occasion, he murdered a man in Montana for his gold, and of other criminal deeds. I did not, however, take much stock in these stories, for Donovan seemed to want to impress upon me the idea that he was one of the most desperate of criminals and the hero of many a black deed.

As they talked the next day about their near escape, Valentine proffered his cell mate with a new ruse. Unless they got out of the jail very soon, pressed the detective, a requisition from the Governor of Indiana might destroy their chances of ever getting away together. That evening the sheriff brought them some newspapers containing an account of Leighton's death. Donovan said nothing except to curse the articles; however, the following morning he offered to tell Valentine "the real facts in the case"...the facts as they appear at the beginning of this chapter.

A CHANGE IN VENUE

When the Second Judicial District Court of Sweetwater County convened that Fall, its grand jury indicted Donovan, but his attorney obtained a change of venue to neighboring

Carbon County for trial. On October 3, 1883, Sheriff Vickery escorted Donovan via train to Rawlins, the Carbon County seat, arriving there at noon.

Nearly a week later, following his arraignment, Donovan applied for new counsel, and the court assigned G.C. Smith to defend him. Not surprisingly, a number of qualified persons declined to serve on a jury which required them to sit in judgment of a man they did not know, in a county in which he had not lived. Consequently, the court and attorneys culled through more than one hundred candidates before selecting a qualified jury.

THE DISTRICT COURT OF
CARBON COUNTY CONVENES

The trial finally got underway on Thursday, October 11, in the newly constructed Carbon County Courthouse. From the start, Donovan's alibi seemed to melt as Attorney Smith called to the stand defense witnesses only to have them deny his client's claims. Although most of the substantive evidence came from Donovan's alleged confession to Detective Valentine, at least one other person heard substantially the same admission: Adam Story. The old man, serving time for contempt of the Sweetwater County Justice of the Peace court, claimed that when the two were alone together, he asked Donovan:

> *"What are you in here for?"*
> *"Nothing at all."*
> *"For nothing at all?"*
> *"Well, I was put in here for killing a man."*
> *"What did you kill him for?"*

"For his money."
"How much did you get?"
"One hundred and twenty-seven dollars."

The hammer, too, came back to haunt Donovan. Witnesses proved that on the day prior to the murder George Hunter and Donovan attempted to use that same implement to repair a roof, although its broken handle prevented its use. Donovan knew where to find it after it had been thrown down behind some barrels in the yard where they worked. And Valentine disclosed that Donovan also admitted twice lighting matches under the bed the night of the murder. That evidence became particularly damaging when the jury learned that Valentine had not visited the crime scene prior to relating Donovan's confession. When reliable witnesses subsequently searched the site, "they found two matches partially burned under the bed."

So, as the evidence—although circumstantial—took shape, the jury had little difficulty imagining the brutal scenarios as they watched the muscular young man, weighing at least 170 pounds, testify.

JUSTICE IN BALANCE

The jury finally received the case on October 17. As Deputy Sheriff Daley escorted the prisoner back to his cell following Judge Parks's charge of responsibilities to the jury, Donovan fatalistically acknowledged, "That settles it."

Three days later, at 6:30 P.M., the jurors sent word to the judge that they had reached a decision. The news quickly spread through town, and the courtroom filled to capacity as people rushed there to hear the verdict. After the jury

The turreted stone building at the upper left is the Carbon County Courthouse in Rawlins, Wyoming, which witnessed many of the most publicized, outrageous trials in the history of Wyoming. (Courtesy Wyoming Division of Cultural Resources)

filed in and the prisoner returned from the jail, the judge called the court to order. Then, as the great room became quiet as poor Bill Leighton's tomb, the jury foreman declared Donovan "Guilty of murder in the first degree."

On October 23, at 4 P.M., another large crowd gathered at the Carbon County Courthouse to hear the judge pronounce his sentence. "The Prisoner walked very erect," reported the local newspaper, "with a springy elastic step when brought into court. After being seated...he appeared somewhat nervous, picked at his trousers and caressed a two weeks old mustachios [*sic*]." The judge reminded him of the jury's decision and asked Donovan if he had anything to say as to why the sentence should not be pronounced. When the prisoner said he did not, the judge said:

> *I do not know as I can say anything to you at this time that would be of benefit to you. You have had a fair trial...the crime you have been convicted of is not an ordinary murder committed in the heat of passion, but murder in the worst form, coolly and deliberately perpetrated. You killed your friend and benefactor in the dead of night while he was asleep. It is not murder. It is assassination.*

As the judge spoke, "the prisoner stood looking at him with something of a sinister expression of countenance, apparently not realizing the terrible position he was in, or, if he did, meeting it with a bravado as brazen as it was astonishing." The judge continued:

> *It is therefore considered by the Court that you, Leroy Donovan, otherwise called "John Lee," be taken hence to the jail of Carbon County, Wyoming Territory, provided*

*by law, and there between the hours of 10 o'clock in the
forenoon and four o'clock in the afternoon, be hung by
the neck until you are dead.*

Attorney John Wesley Blake, who had been appointed
by the court to replace the less experienced Smith, promptly
applied to the Wyoming Supreme Court for a writ of errors.

Donovan took the harsh, but unsurprising, news without expression or any trace of emotion. Deputies immediately returned him to his cell downstairs in the county jail
where, before becoming absorbed in a novel, he asked a visitor to "Tell the boys at Green River that I am doing first rate
here and have plenty of grub."

IN THE HANDS OF THE SUPREME COURT

As the final days of 1883 slipped past, Donovan
remained optimistic that the Supreme Court would grant
him a new trial so that he could call additional witnesses to
testify in his behalf. He remained so upbeat, in fact, that
when M.D. Houghton, the local photographer, came to
take his picture, Donovan "appeared to be very much
amused at the operation and requested some copies of the
photograph when completed to send to his relations in
Washington Territory." By the second week of December,
when Donovan's mother came to see him, that attitude had
changed. In fact, witnesses claimed they saw the prisoner
"completely breaking down and copiously shedding tears."

In the meantime, even though Blake became the Carbon County Attorney and Prosecutor, he remained supportive of his former client and even appealed to Governor
William Hale to intercede by granting a stay of sentence for

The Carbon County Courtroom (circa 1910) hosted the trials of two of the most senseless crimes ever committed in the Wyoming Territory. The first involved John Leroy Donovan, the clawhammer assassin, while the second saw drunken Ben Carter, the "Badman from Bitter Creek," unsuccessfully plead his case. (Courtesy Wyoming Division of Cultural Resources)

Donovan. The Governor, after formal and deliberate consideration, however, supported the Supreme Court on every point of contention. Further, he advised Blake that Donovan's mother visited the Capitol and that he received a number of letters from the condemned man's family. While he understood their anxiety, said the Governor, neither his sympathy "or their grief can furnish any guide...in the performance of so grave a duty and responsibility." Would the Governor intercede in Donovan's behalf? In a word, "No."

THE FINAL HOURS

The day before Donovan's execution, he received a number of visitors and spent the greater part of the day reading the Bible in his cell at the Carbon County jail. But that night, he seemed to sleep well as William Casto and Tom Maloney quietly carried out the death watch with him.

Rising early the morning of January 18, 1884, the prisoner "made his toilet with considerable care" before eating a hearty breakfast of toast, eggs, and coffee. His favorite cigarette followed that last meal. At 8 A.M. Donovan's spiritual advisor, Catholic priest Father Cassidy, joined him in his cell. Still later, if not ebullient, the prisoner apparently held no grudges because he took time to bid farewell to Sheriff I.C. [Isaac Carson] Miller of Rawlins and to thank him for his kind and generous treatment during his incarceration.

No less than two hours later, ten guards responded to keep back the crowd of approximately three hundred people who gathered around the jail hoping unsuccessfully to get inside the area where the gallows had been constructed the previous week. There in a corner on the east side of the jail, where it met the courthouse, a fourteen-foot-by-ten-foot pen, with eighteen-foot high walls, protected the gallows tree from outside view. A board fence concealed the pathway from the rear door of the jail to the scaffold.

With official permission, Donovan's mother met with him for the last time in an emotional scene at 10:30 A.M. Mrs. Donovan seemed more visibly moved by the experience than her condemned son. After only fifteen minutes alone together, the authorities let those persons who were still in the courthouse parade through the corridor to ogle the mother and son as they counted down the final minutes toward his execution. Finally, the lawmen escorted all but Donovan himself and authorized execution witnesses from the building.

The court appointed John Wesley Blake to provide a legal defense for murderer John Leroy Donovan. Although forced to quit his client following his election as Attorney and Prosecutor for Carbon County, Blake remained supportive and even appealed to Governor William Hale to stay Donovan's sentence. (Courtesy Wyoming Division of Cultural Resources)

At 11:15 A.M., Mrs. Donovan bid her son farewell as Sheriff Miller and Father Cassidy quietly led the doomed man, clad in carpet slippers, gray jeans, black coat, and collared, but tieless, white shirt, from his cell and to the gallows. Those who witnessed the solemnity of that last trek described it as "terrible."

With his arms bound, Donovan walked firmly, without a tremor or falter, on to the trapdoor of the scaffold. At the "hanging tree," Father Cassidy offered a prayer after which the prisoner repeated the priest's responses and kissed the crucifix. "Do you have anything to say?" the sheriff asked. Donovan replied in a voice clear and firm, "I have nothing to say, only I did not have a fair trial. If I had I could have proved myself innocent." With that final exchange, the sheriff slipped the traditional black hood over his head at precisely 11:26 A.M., while firmly binding his arms and his ankles. The lawman also carefully adjusted the twisted sea grass knot of the noose at the base of his skull so as to snap the spine at the moment of impact, thus ensuring a swift and painless death.

"Is the rope too tight?" asked the sheriff. In a firm, easy tone, Donovan replied, "It is as tight as it can be without choking me."

Two minutes later, the sheriff stepped back and pulled the trap release cord. Donovan immediately dropped some six feet with a dull thud. Other than a slight tremor, the body hung motionless. Three minutes later, Donovan's knees convulsively pulled up, this being the only other movement of his body before the assigned photographer "Artist" Johnson took a picture of the suspended corpse. At

11:45 A.M., officials removed the black cap, but waited ten minutes more before they cut down the body. Doctors Stover and Woodruff pronounced Donovan dead. After Coroner Edgerton officially evaluated the body, the court empaneled a jury which pronounced:

We do find that the deceased came to his death by being hanged by the neck by the proper authorities, under an order from the court as shown by the sheriff of Carbon County, in evidence during the trial.

Undertaker Daley then placed the body in a casket before delivering it to Donovan's mother, who subsequently took it to Hailey, Idaho, for burial.

POSTSCRIPT

The day before his death, Donovan penned the following surprisingly sensitive and articulate letter to Mrs. Wesley S. Cox, who brought "little delicacies" several times to him in his cell after his sentencing and even sent him a note concerning his "spiritual welfare."

My Kind Friend:—Your kind and encouraging letter of the 16th inst. [only two days before his execution] *was handed to me by Sheriff Miller yesterday, and I deem it my duty to write and express my gratitude to you for your kindness to me, which words fail to do on paper. As your letter is of that nature which has always been foreign to me, as I have been a herdsman the majority of my life, home, love and affection I never knew, and to receive the loving blessings and good will from a true, loving and noble woman, as you are, fills my heart with an unexplainable gratitude that belongs*

These young ladies contemplate a bleak, barren vista from a hill out-side the mining town of Rock Springs, Wyoming (circa 1888-90). (Courtesy Wyoming Division of Cultural Resources)

only to the purest of people and hearts as yours, and your kind, mother blessing that you have wished me shall be among my last thoughts, as I die an innocent man. I am not guilty of the crime I am charged with. I shall send your kind letter to my sister who will thank you with her whole heart for your last kind words of comfort to her brother.

(Signed) John L. Donovan

SOURCES CITED

An in-depth telling of this story was only possible through the careful study of Carbon County Criminal Case File #171, the Wyoming Supreme Court Case File #2-15, and Volume III of *Reports of Cases Argued and Determined in the Supreme Court of the Territory of Wyoming and the Supreme Court of the State of Wyoming* (St. Paul, Minnesota: West Publishing Company, 1893) these documents are on file at the Wyoming State Archives.

Ancillary sources, such as the 1880 *Wyoming Census* and such periodicals as the *Carbon County Journal*, the *Cheyenne Sun,* and *Cheyenne Daily Leader,* also provided a host of relevant details not found elsewhere.

George Cooke

You are Respectfully Invited to Attend my Execution

> ... *Try the murderer, convict him and then*
> *hang him as soon as possible. It is high time*
> *Wyoming should begin to punish criminals.*
> LARAMIE WEEKLY SENTINEL,
> *1 DECEMBER 1883*

GEORGE COOKE, A thirty-year-old immigrant from Worcester, England, faced the harsh sentiment expressed in the above article two days after he fired a lead bullet deep into the brain of his brother-in-law James Blount.

Regrettably, Cooke killed the East Side school janitor in Laramie. Even worse, he committed a "murder most foul, perpetrated through the influence and at the instigation of drink." And it happened on Thanksgiving, a time when any God-fearing man should have praised the good Lord for his blessings. And few felt stronger about such conduct than J.H. Hayford, the editor of the *Laramie Weekly Sentinel*; Herman V.S. Groesbeck, the Albany County Justice of the Peace; Jacob B. Blair, the Associate Justice of the Wyoming Supreme Court as well as judge of the Second Judicial District Court;

and most particularly, Governor William Hale. These men, in word if not in deed, preached that intemperance and those who indulged in it were only slightly less evil than the devil himself. Unfortunately, like most politicians of past and present, they seemed more interested in pontificating than in creating a climate that might prevent such sins.

THANKSGIVING PLANS GET SIDETRACKED

Murderers should be tried by competent courts and then hung by competent officers.

LARAMIE WEEKLY SENTINEL,
1 DECEMBER 1883

When Cooke came to America in 1876, he worked for some Laramie area ranchers and claimed he acquired his taste for alcohol while employed as a cowpuncher. The young Englishman later became a Union Pacific Railroad coal heaver and ostler [a man who tended engines at the end of their runs] at the Medicine Bow roundhouse. And he seemed to do well in that position until November 28, 1883, when he hopped a late freight to Laramie City to spend at least part of the following day—Thanksgiving—with his infirm, sixty-eight-year-old mother, Mary Ann. Other family members who planned to attend that event included his sister, who was named for her mother; her husband, James Blount; their son, "Little Sammy," plus their new baby girl, born just three days earlier. At least Cooke said he planned to visit those folks the night he boarded that train.

Arriving in Laramie City about 5:15 A.M—too early for a social call on his relatives—he went first to the Humboldt House to prime his pump with a couple of beers. After all, he

George Cooke, a part-time railroad coal loader and full-time sot, became the fourth man to be legally executed in Wyoming Territory when he shot to death his brother-in-law on Thanksgiving Day in 1883. (Sketch by Eileen Hayes Skibo)

had not had a drink since just before leaving Medicine Bow about ten hours earlier. Then he went on to John Grover's saloon. He might have had breakfast there if he had been feeling better, but he believed he really needed another drink.

Later that morning, he stopped by Jesse Converse's shop to pick up the Colt .45 revolver with a sawed-off barrel that he left there for repair during a previous trip. Converse, a gunsmith and jeweler, replaced a missing screw and fixed a faulty trigger spring in the old double-action revolver. Finally, about mid-morning, after putting away at least a quart of gin and whiskey, Cooke linked up with his brother Albert and brother-in-law Blount. The trio almost immediately started making the rounds of the local grog shops while drinking and arguing over real and imagined troubles. Fired by liquor, Blount, "a large, heartily built man" of about 175 pounds, threatened well and often that day to whip his smaller in-law. Cooke, on the other hand, made no bones about the fact that if Blount laid his ham-like hands on him, Cooke would kill him. They had argued regularly almost from the time his sister Mary Ann married Blount, whom many considered to be "a shiftless sort of fellow who was principally supported by his wife."

Early that evening, armed with his pistol, a belly full of beer, and a variety of other libations, Cooke went looking for trouble. He found it first in the Union Pacific oil room, where the employees there later claimed he robbed, but did not harm, them. Witnesses next saw Cooke about 6:30 P.M. in Cleveland's Saloon, where he pulled his gun, saying that he planned to kill Blount. About thirty minutes later, Cooke appeared "a little under the influence of liquor," drinking with two other men in J. Fred Hesse's saloon at 117 Front

Street. Hesse later testified he did not know the men with Cooke, but he heard the young drunk invite them to dinner. They left together, he said. Everything seemed amicable enough until the men unexpectedly met Blount just two doors down from Hesse's, in front of L. Rudolph Abrams's saloon. Cooke's sharp tongue immediately lashed his brother-in-law who, despite his physical dominance, tried to calm Cooke with a proffered drink. Neither man needed a fight at that particular point, and Cooke's companions, sensing trouble, scattered like quail. With the fuse lit and threats exchanged, Cooke pulled his pistol from his pocket and fired point-blank into Blount's brain. The blast of gun powder left a raw, black burn where the bullet entered the victim's left cheek. Death followed instantaneously.

As the sharp report rang in his alcohol-numbed ears, Cooke saw the forty-year-old Blount crash to the ground, his head propped against the doorway step with his feet stretched between the end poles of the horse hitch near the street.

A Boy Saw It All

If Blount, in that last nano-second, thought only God witnessed the crime, he was wrong. Dead wrong. Fifteen-year-old Henry N. Brodie, astride his borrowed, black, bare-back mount only about thirty feet from the murder, saw it all. The boy later testified that, while awaiting his father, Anthony T. Brodie, who had gone into Hesse's for a brew about five minutes earlier with his friend Hugh Lavery, he saw Cooke come out of the saloon and say:

"What are you doing with this horse?" I did not answer him. He then went back into Mr. Hesse's saloon.

James H. Hayford, the puritanical publisher and editor of the Laramie Weekly Sentinel, *made clear his views about "justice" and the legal system when he editorially took to task the accused George Cooke: "Try the murderer, convict him and then hang him as soon as possible."* (Courtesy Wyoming Division of Cultural Resources)

He came out again with two other men. Did not know the men. Cook [sic] then walked down past Abrams' Saloon and a man [Blount] came out of Abrams' Saloon. Did not know this man at the time.

Next, two men stood there a little time...Then the man [Blount]...said, "Well, never mind, George. Let it all pass. Come in and have a drink." Cook would not go in and kept on sassing him...The man said to George Cook, "I've a mind to shoot your nose." Cook, stepping back, said, "Do you mean it?" The man said, "Yes." Cook said, "Do you mean it?" Then before the man could answer, George Cook pulled his pistol, stepped forward and shot him. Cook had the pistol in his right side pocket.

Cook put the pistol almost up to the other man's face. The man fell as soon as the shot was fired. He shot the man in the face. The light was shining from the windows at Abrams and the bakery shop.

After shooting, he walked around to the man's head and said, "Did I kill you?" Cook then ran out into the road towards the Express Office.

Indeed. He ran west down the middle of the street then turned north where he met William Brown and Michael A. Watters as they walked south toward the saloon. Cooke stopped, held them at bay with his wavering gun, and in a low, almost imperceptible voice warned, "Damn you, don't come here." Stepping off the sidewalk into the street, Brown and Watters eased past Cooke, who, dressed in a navy blue shirt, vest, and coat, vanished into the cold November night.

Shortly after 8 P.M., near the mill at the foot of North B Street, Cooke met Frank Fagan, another fifteen-year-old. He warned the lad that he had shot a man and he planned to sleep in the mill. "Cook [*sic*]," according to Fagan, "pulled out a pistol and said, 'See that,' and told me to go on. He was pretty drunk and seemed as if he had been running before he came up to me." Cooke then entered the mill, lay down, and tried fitfully to sleep off his drunk, but rest escaped him. Sometime during the wee hours, still muddled, he arose. It is not known whether conscience or self-preservation took over, but he went outside and threw his pistol away.

FROM HANGOVER TO HANGMAN

The poor stricken widow and orphans of the murdered Blunt [sic] *have the full sympathy of our people. Their wretchedness cries to heaven for the redress of the wrongs they suffer.*

LARAMIE WEEKLY SENTINEL
1 DECEMBER *1883*

Cooke spent the rest of that night wandering the back alleys and side streets until dawn found him, still in a stupor, lying on the Laramie River bank near a bridge. About 7:30 A.M., he headed for the railroad tracks, where he met a brakeman about to board an outbound train. As he talked to the railway man, law officer Henry Smith approached and asked, "George, you know what you done last night?"

"Is Blount dead?"

"Yes! Dead as a door-nail."

"My God! Would I shoot my own relation...I am very sorry for it."

But when Smith asked if he had a gun, Cooke replied wishfully that if he had his revolver and could get as far as

Medicine Bow, he would get horses there and no one would ever catch him. Before any such opportunity arose, however, Smith put the placid Cooke under arrest. Following a brief "Goodbye" stop at the house of Cooke's brother Albert, Smith and his prisoner continued to the local jail where Deputy Sheriff James Sterling's wife, with a babe in arms, did the honors of locking up the murderer.

On Friday, November 30, Dr. J.H. Finfrock, with the help of Dr. P.F. Gunsler, conducted an autopsy on Blount's body. Late that morning, physicians extracted a "battered and flattened" lead slug that lodged against the back of the victim's skull. At the Coroner's Inquest held four hours later, testimony by the various witnesses endorsed the key facts already disclosed by the examining physicians. Ed N. Allen, a thirty-five year-old barkeep at Grover's saloon, for example, recalled seeing Blount and the Cooke brothers drinking in his saloon that Thanksgiving Day. Still others testified that Blount, at one point, pulled off his coat and threatened, "I...can whip any man in Laramie City!" A witness said Cooke responded, "Damn you. I'll take my six-shooter and shoot your damned toes off and will kill you!" Fortunately, two or three bystanders stepped between them before serious damage ensued. Based upon the evidence presented at that inquest, authorities charged Cooke with murder.

In the meantime, a reporter from the local newspaper visited Cooke in his cell. The accused man "broke down completely...and said...that he was drunk, and had no knowledge of what he had done until arrested; that Blunt [*sic*] was the best friend he ever had, and it was he who had brought him to this country six years ago."

"...DEAD! DEAD! DEAD!"

The enormity of this crime shocks every nobler [sic]
nature, and its commission adds but another count to
the long indictment against liquor traffic, which awaits
the verdict of the people and the sentence of law. The
blood of a father; the wailing of the widow; the cry of
the orphan; the sorrow of the mother, are louder than
our voice; mightier than our pen. Is there a whisky sell-
er who cannot hear them ringing in his ears? As we
stand beside the coffin of poor Blunt [sic], *and lift*
from his ghastly wound the crimson covering we would
hold it up to heaven before this people, and in the
name of Isreal [sic] *God, ask: 'Is it not enough?'*

LARAMIE WEEKLY SENTINEL
1 DECEMBER 1883

On Monday, December 3, the court empaneled a special
grand jury and brought an indictment against Cooke before
issuing a venire for a special petit jury that convened the following Friday morning.

Court and other legal officials railed against Wyoming's
newsmen, most especially those in Albany County, for so
prejudicing the public that 118 potential jurors had to be dismissed before twelve good and able citizens could be found to
sit in judgment. They charged, too, that the media so
inflamed the local populace that it hanged Cooke in effigy
and endangered his chance for a fair trial.

Despite his published words to the contrary, the
Laramie Weekly Sentinel's Hayford defended his editorial passion by pontificating:

We believe the Sentinel expressed no opinion as to the
guilt or innocence of Cooke, and merely gave a brief

account of the homicide as it was currently reported. The Boomerang [a rival Laramie newspaper] *did charge it as an entirely wilful and malicious murder; tried and condemned the accused, and did its best to excite a mob to execute him. This was a very foolish and unwise thing to do.*

In words that many believe echo the plight of today's legal system, the *Sentinel's* editor further charged that the law is "framed to protect instead of punish criminals. Nobody doubts but any one of the 100 of those jurymen who were excused would have given the accused a fair and impartial trial." Continuing his tirade, Hayford said:

But the fact is no man who is guilty of a crime wants a fair and impartial trial and to have exact justice done him. His object is to defeat the ends of justice, and by the ingenuity of shrewd lawyers and under the existing laws he is generally able to accomplish this.

During the trial that followed on December 7, the prosecution laid out a clear chain of evidence to prove that Cooke shot poor Blount. Although the killer's attorneys, William J. McIntyre and Stephen W. Downey, tried to counter that their client "was irresponsible for his acts by being crazy drunk...and, thus, incapable of 'premeditation' and 'malice aforethought,'" that strategy failed as the jurors pronounced their verdict. Calling the court to order, a bailiff brought Cooke before the bar where he heard Justice Blair, in his capacity as Judge of the Second Judicial District Court, say, "You have been indicted in this court for having wilfully, deliberately and premeditatedly, with malice aforethought, taken the life of James Blount, within the jurisdiction of this court." But before pronouncing sentence, the judge asked, "Have you anything to say why the sentence of the court should not be pronounced upon you?" In reply, Cooke said in a low, tremulous voice, "I have only to say that I am not guilty. I don't know how James Blount came to his death, and don't think I have had a fair trial." The alcohol apparently so pickled his brain that it affected his short-term memory, because he later recalled his crime.

Apparently more interested in saving Cooke's soul than sparing his life, the judge launched a florid sermon that, by comparison, must have made the sentencing itself seem tolerable even to poor Cooke. Thankfully, if not mercifully, the judge concluded his seemingly endless tirade with, "...that you, George Cook [*sic*], then and there, by said sheriff [be] hanged by the neck until you are dead!...dead!...dead!"

A Time to Reflect

In a desperate fight against time—and intolerance—Cooke's attorneys filed a bill of exception with the Wyoming Supreme Court, but that plea for a new trial fell on deaf ears.

As time slipped away, several reporters from the *Laramie Weekly Sentinel* visited Cooke on New Year's Day 1884, in his "dark and gloomy" cell. There, in the basement of the Albany County Courthouse, the following interview took place:

> *How are you passing the time?*
> *Oh, pretty well.*
> *Do you get lonesome?*

The Albany County Courthouse, completed January 1872 as the first permanent courthouse in Wyoming, served for sixty years. The impos- ing red stone and brick building housed the county jail in the basement and various county offices and vaults for records storage occupied the first floor. The second story contained a spacious courtroom and jury rooms. Regrettably, wind damaged the cupola atop the roof and it had to be removed in 1883. (Courtesy Wyoming Division of Cultural Resources)

Oh, not much. This is a pretty jolly place.
How do you pass the time?
Well, I read till I get tired and then walk about.
What do you read?
Oh, something jolly.
*Would you prefer the Days Doings, Police Gazette
and such like papers?*
Yes, they make first-rate reading.

According to Sheriff Louis Miller, who authorized the visit and interview, Cooke, indeed, took his jail time in stride by singing, telling obscene stories, and reading a variety of papers and periodicals.

As the determined newsmen tried to make Cooke realize his precarious future, the condemned man said, he "supposed he killed Blunt [*sic*], but that he did not feel so badly about it as he should have if he had not been drunk." The interview continued:

But who was to blame for your being drunk?
*I suppose I was, but I did not have a fair trial, and
there have been a half dozen worse cases than mine and
nobody hung for it.*

Cooke asked, "with a little show of solicitude," if the reporters did not think the sentence of hanging might be reduced to imprisonment. "Very doubtful," they replied. Then the reporters asked:

*Do not the circumstances in which you are placed
turn your thoughts to the future?*
Well, I haven't thought much about it.
*Have you no convictions or ideas as to the future
existence?*

This Albany County Courtroom in Laramie, Wyoming, witnessed two of the most notorious murder cases in Wyoming's territorial history. In 1884—two years before this picture—the court sentenced George Cooke to death for killing his brother-in-law outside a Laramie City saloon. That same fate fell four years later to George Black for the spiteful killing of an old hermit who lived near Pole Mountain. Here, too, in March 1870, women served for the first time in recorded history as jurors. (Courtesy Wyoming Division of Cultural Resources)

Not much.

Don't you think the life you have led in the past and its awful results ought to make you wish to change your course and try to seek forgiveness for the past and lead a different life in the future, whether you are to live or die?

Well, I suppose so.

Their note pads chocked full of quotes as banal and pointless as their subsequent rhetoric and proselytizing, the newsmen filed their stories. "We left him [Cooke]," they wrote "feeling that we never before saw or heard of such an entire absence of all moral sensibility, of all idea of right or wrong, in any human being," reported the newsmen. "He did not seem disposed to admit that he had done anything seriously wrong, or that he ought to be punished much or any, or that he felt any reservation regarding the past or any need for reformation for the future. He furnishes typical illustration of what whisky can do for a man."

SUPREME COURT DENIES RETRIAL

Thursday evening's tragedy cries aloud for the avenging hand of justice. Let the Christian people and temperance reformers of Laramie—men and women—rise up in their might and majesty, and show that there is a God in Isreal [sic].

LARAMIE WEEKLY SENTINEL
1 DECEMBER 1883

Or, as the reporters later wrote:

The Supreme Court this week overruled the motion for a new trial in the Cooke murder case, and fixed the time for his execution on the 12th of December next [1884].

Probably public sentiment will generally endorse this action of the court. There is a general feeling that it is time an example was made of some of these murderers, and there could scarce be a more suitable subject than this man Cooke. He is the most stolid and brutal, the most lacking in sensibility of any human being we ever saw. We have never heard of or seen him manifest any compunction, sorrow or regret at the cold-blooded murder he committed. If hanging him will have a tendency to check the promiscuous shooting so common in this country, it will be the best use to which he can be put.

As Wyoming's long, lonely winter set in and Cooke's life grew as short as the shrinking, sunlit days, the condemned man made a futile attempt to escape. He sawed off his ankle shackles with the nicked blade of a case knife; however, a fellow prisoner warned Sheriff Miller in time to thwart Cooke's attempt to cheat the hangman. Toward the end of November, Cooke's mother finally gave up hope and with the charitable support of friends and acquaintances, she planned to return to her home in England. "I can't stay here," she weeped, "while my boy is hanged."

Three days before his execution, the now contrite Cooke wrote to Blount's widow—his sister—and expressed sorrow for his crime. He even asked her forgiveness, but Mary Ann at first refused. Nor would she visit him, because she "could not endure the added agony to that which she had suffered before." Later, changing her mind, she sent word that she forgave him for her husband's slaying and hoped "that he would be forgiven in the hereafter."

On Thursday, December 11—the night before his execution—Cooke, in stockinged feet and flame-red, flannel underwear sat in his eight-foot by ten-foot cage which opened out into a little passageway. It, in turn, was separated from the pathway through which visitors entered by heavily latticed iron work that extended to the ceiling of the jail. Those uninvited guests hovered there like buzzards at the door to his cell hoping to catch some last carrion comments that might drop from his lips. Despite those efforts, Cooke thwarted their attempts, vowing no final public statement until the next day. He was cool and self-possessed; the only hint of anxiety was his chain smoking of cigarettes. Still, that didn't stop reporters from trying to tempt him with more mundane conversation. They still hoped that the condemned man might change his mind and offer some quotable quote. "Cook [*sic*], you are looking well," one reporter commented. "I have been growing fat for some time, and will be fat enough to kill tomorrow," he laughingly replied. When pressed to explain how he felt, Cooke said he had made his "peace with his God" and that he expected he would "go to a better world."

Failing to get something more interesting, a *Cheyenne Democratic Leader* newsman opted instead to describe Cooke's physical appearance: "...about five-foot, ten-inches, well built and about 160 pounds. He has light hair of that peculiar color often called 'sandy'. He wears a light beard, and is looking pale, the result of his long confinement, no doubt."

Finally, about 11:10 P.M., Cooke crawled into the slim bunk affixed to the iron wall of the small cell and snuggled under his blanket. Less than five minutes later, he seemed to fall asleep. According to those who participated in his death watch, Cooke's slumber continued, although he "turned over uneasily" in his bed about 2:10 A.M.

About 8 A.M. on his final day, he awoke and donned the blue suit pants, white collarless shirt, and new shoes that he selected for the occasion. The sun shined brightly through the sharp December air. A deputy brought the hearty meal Cooke especially requested to his cell: a dozen soft boiled eggs, beef steak, chicken, a big bunch of celery, a generous quantity of bread, and two large cups of coffee. Those who saw him said later he seemed resigned to his fate. By the time Father Cumminskey arrived to hear his confession and confer his blessings, Cooke had grown quite serious. The indifference and bravado, previously perceived by the press, "had entirely disappeared." After the priest left, the sheriff opened the doors of the jail to the general public as some two-hundred people filed down the narrow stairway and into the basement. There, they took a last, or in many cases a first, glimpse at the doomed man. Cooke, in his shirt sleeves, seemed to take the "circus" in good spirits as he stood behind the metal grate. In fact, he spoke briefly to those he knew and grasped the fingers of several visitors who reached through the metal work as a gesture of farewell. Two ladies in the group wept as they gave him a small bouquet. Trying to break the tension, he eased them by saying, "Now don't go home and hold your thumbs in your mouths and cry. I'm all right."

INVITATION TO AN EXECUTION

Specifically prepared for that purpose, the two-story execution shed, some twenty feet square, consisted of boards set up on end with the cracks battened to prevent sneak peeks by the curious. The structure had a trap or drop door in the middle floor. Of the twenty-five to thirty people invited to witness the execution, most included officials, members of the jury, physicians, clergymen, and members of the press. Alas, by law Cooke was given the dubious privilege of inviting an additional half-dozen friends and acquaintances, so he sent the following invitation in his own handwriting:

Dear Sir:—You are respectfully invited to attend my execution December 12, A.D. 1884, at 11 o'clock A.M. *at the Court House in the City of Laramie. Yours, Respectfully...*

[signed] *George Cooke*

Cooke continued to maintain his composure right up to the time of his execution. Father Cumminskey, who stayed with him during that final hour, led the way to the gallows as Sheriff Miller and Deputy Sheriff James Sterling walked at each side of Cooke. Finally, at the scaffold, the condemned man walked up the stairs with firm, steady steps, with no assistance, or apparent nervousness. Following a brief informal, religious service, the sheriff asked Cooke if he had any final words. "I have not," the prisoner replied before stepping onto the drop door. After pinioning the prisoner's arms and legs, the sheriff adjusted the noose so the knot lay at the base of the left ear. Only moments later at precisely 11:26 A.M., after the black velvet cap was slipped down over Cooke's head, the trap fell open with a loud "bang." Cooke's neck snapped at the end of a six foot fall. Little involuntary muscular contraction followed, and within four minutes, his pulse could no longer be detected. Eleven minutes after that a physician pronounced him dead. Clasped in Cooke's lifeless hand the doctor found a small crucifix that Father Cumminskey had pressed into his palm during their farewell handshake.

After cutting down the body at 11: 45 A.M. and placing it in a plain coffin, officials took it to the local Catholic cemetery for burial, his relatives having declined to take charge of it.

A FINAL FORK IN THE CORPSE

Let punishment—sure and swift—be meted out to the drunken craven who shot down an unarmed man in cold blood, and then 'held up' two peaceable pedestrians at the jeopardy of their lives.

LARAMIE WEEKLY SENTINEL

1 DECEMBER 1883

Editor Hayford, whose pen helped prod the alcoholic Cooke up the gallows steps, lacked the intestinal fortitude to witness the product of his preaching. Although invited to attend the execution, he "found a substitute and declined." Still, he could not suppress sticking this final fork in Cooke's cold corpse:

Another victim has been sacrificed upon the altar of rum. If it shall serve to help arouse public sentiment to drive the monster evil from the land; if it shall operate as a warning against the carrying of deadly weapons and the reckless taking of human life, George Cook [sic] *will not have died in vain.*

SOURCES CITED

This story, like all the others in this book, relies most heavily upon details contained in the primary source documents, most particularly the criminal case files which, in this instance, is the Albany County Second Judicial Court Criminal Case File #181 at the Wyoming State Archives. Interestingly, although nearly every source identifies Cooke as "Cook," the young murderer clearly signed his last name with an "e." The curious will find at least two examples of his true signature affixed to original documents in the aforementioned criminal case file. The first appears on a "Plea to the Jurisdiction of the Court" (6 December 1883) and the second is on an "Affidavit of George Cook [*sic*] that he is a poor person."

Additional important research sources of that time included the *Laramie Weekly Sentinel* and the *Boomerang*, published in Laramie, as well as the *Daily Sun* and *Democrat Leader* in Cheyenne. Two other sources that provided limited, but important, corroborative information are the *Wyoming Tribune* of Rawlins plus Gladys B. Beery's *Real West* article entitled, "He Died Game" (October 1983).

John Owens

Dinner With the Devil

"YAH," JOSHED JACOB Schmerer to anyone who asked him about his bachelor status, "if I could find some good German voman who knew how to vork and how to cook I vould marry. But these American vimmens vant the men to do all the work."

Too bad fifty-six-year-old Jake didn't look harder. A wife—even one of those "American vimmens"—would have been a much better extra hand than the deadly partner he chose. Safer too. But when the Johnson County pioneer hired twenty-four-year-old John Owens, alias "Bill Booth," to help him hay, the clean-cut youth seemed an able enough worker. Owens, too, seemed happy with the arrangement. The young man needed the money and a place to stay. Jake wanted someone to help him hunt and aid with the chores at his place in the Red Hills six to eight miles southeast of Buffalo on Dry Creek. The large house, barn, and stable needed tending. Jake's cows, saddle pony, and a team of horses, one large bay and one buckskin with a four-inch wide black streak that went from withers to tail, also required care. And, of course, it would be nice to have some company—someone to talk to—on those long, lonely Wyoming nights.

In fact, it seemed to be a pretty good arrangement for both of them until Burrill Madden, a neighbor known locally as "Nigger Steve," noticed a strange lack of activity at Jake's place. During subsequent testimony in late June 1884 at the Second Judicial District Court trial in Buffalo, he recalled last visiting Jake on Tuesday, March 25, 1884. The old German sat, dressed in a "striped woolen shirt and plain pants, sewing at a table in his cabin about 4:30 in the afternoon." He wore shoes, too. At least he had them on his feet the last time the "colored gentleman" saw Jake...alive.

AN UNEXPECTED VISIT

Shortly after 11 A.M. the following day—Wednesday, March 26—Owens showed up unexpectedly at the small coal mine where Madden worked near his cabin. The surprised Madden had not seen the young man since Schmerer "paid off" Owens last fall. Regardless, Madden welcomed the unexpected visitor because he had no chewing tobacco and Owens had a plug to share. Inviting his company to lunch, Madden inquired about Owens's old employer. The young man said Jake had gone down to Crazy Woman Creek with a man from Prairie Dog who promised to bring

John Owens, perhaps best known as "Bill Booth," chopped short with a hatchet the life of an old Johnson County German settler. The callous Owens paid for that crime when, with his head in a noose, he met his Maker near the County Courthouse in Buffalo, Wyoming, on March 5, 1886. (Sketch by Eileen Hayes Skibo)

him home in his wagon after they bought some chickens. But Owens assured Madden that Jake had given him the keys to his cabin and told him that he could stay there until he returned.

About 4 P.M. that afternoon, Madden ventured over to Jake's place, where he found Owens in the cabin beating up some batter for slapjacks. After sharing some coffee and a bit of the hotcakes, Madden said he hoped Jake would return soon because he wanted to borrow some supplies. Assured by Owens that the old German would approve, he helped himself to some yeast powder, a box of coffee, and a tin cup of lard before the young man sent Madden on his way.

A winter storm the next day kept Madden close to home. Although he returned to Jake's the following morning, he found the place vacant. About two inches of new snow lay on the ground, but the lack of tracks around the cabin and outbuildings meant that if anyone had been there, they must have gone before the storm. Perhaps Jake and Owens went hunting. The horses and saddles had vanished, too, but the harness still hung on the wall of the barn. Strange. Very strange. The place seemed unusually quiet. Abandoned, in fact.

A Deathly Vacant Ranch

Exactly one week later Madden returned to Jake's place. Peeking into the cabin window, he also saw that Jake's gun and bullet belt no longer lay in the rack above the bed, although a battered hat perched on the bunk. Owens's old gum rubber boots hung from a nail on the wall. Aware that Jake occasionally went on a spree, Madden tempered his concern, but remained suspicious. However, a week later, he still saw no sign of life at his neighbor's cabin. Madden now knew something was wrong. "Dutch," as folks frequently called Jake, might go on a toot, but never for so long a time. Nope, it just didn't seem right! Riding into Buffalo, Madden went directly to the Occidental Hotel where he told an acquaintance, J.M. Lobban, of his concerns. Lobban tried to assure Madden that the old German probably would turn up. But a week later, even Lobban acknowledged the problem and notified Sheriff Frank Canton. The lawman and A.J. McCray, a partner in the Occidental Hotel, jumped into a buggy and went to look around. Jake had been the hotel's first cook shortly after it opened for business in the fall of 1880. Although their search found no evidence of a crime, Madden remained so concerned that he spent nearly every day during the last two weeks of April scouring the hills for Jake...or his body.

SWEET SCENT OF DEATH

Finally about sundown on May 2, as Madden walked through a steep, rock-strewn canyon nearly two miles from Jake's cabin, he caught the sickening sweet scent of death on the wind:

I got a smell of something...I hunted around, but the wind was not exactly right to get where it was, so I left it until the next morning, then I went back to the same place, but the wind was not right. Then I took quite a circle and then came back about 10 A.M. To the mouth of the canon [sic]. The wind was blowing just about right then and I got a scent of it. I followed it up until I run on a dead calf.

Sheriff Frank M. Canton, with members of the Johnson County Coroner's Jury, followed "Nigger Steve" Madden east of Buffalo, Wyoming, into a canyon choked with wild cherry bushes. There, they found Jacob Schmerer's body "pushed under a large...projecting rock...not readily visible." (Courtesy Wyoming Division of Cultural Resources)

I stopped when I came to that, and made up my mind it was what I was smelling. I stood looking at it and started off to go away when I cast my eye upon a big rock hanging over, and then I saw I suppose half a dozen flies. I supposed the flies was flying from this calf as I had seen it was very close, but I went there and threw off four or five rocks and then I could see this man's cloths [sic] *and could see he had on plaid pants, so I just threw the rock back and started to town.*

Madden immediately sought out Dr. John C. Watkins, the Johnson County Coroner. The physician, in turn, had Sheriff Canton quickly subpoena a coroner's jury to conduct an inquest to identify the corpse and determine the cause of death.

The following day Madden led the doctor, sheriff, and members of the jury to where the distinctive plaid pants marked the corpse. They found Jake's body "pushed under a large...projecting rock...not readily visible," in a canyon that was choked with wild cherry bushes. Upon reaching the site, the doctor and Madden tossed the smaller stones off the badly decomposed body so it could be pulled from beneath the boulder. Despite the condition of the corpse, Doctor Watkins immediately recognized his old patient. Not only did he know Jake by his clothes, but he confirmed a cracked rib that he had treated on Jake's right side. "He was bare footed," too, the doctor later testified, and "looked as though they had him lately washed." Doctor Watkins added:

The hands had been eaten some by insects. He had on pants, a woolen shirt, around his head was a coat on the outside with a cord around it; a common cotten [sic] *cord same as is usually used for a clothes line.*

It was fastened around the coat. I cut the cord and took off the coat. Underneath this was a blue jumper or shirt, with some cord tied around that. I cut off this cord, or Mr. Snyder and myself did, and then some cord was tied very tightly around the neck.

I took a stick and examined the head and found it was crushed in three or four places...I passed this stick through from one side all the way through to the other. The brain was all disorganized so there was no trouble in passing the stick through. I also cut open the shirt but found no injuries upon the body. I had the jury examine the body at the same time and see the wounds, which I showed to them, and also that the bones were very much crushed. The jury were then brought into town and also the body and an inquest was held here in the court house, in the room of the Sheriff.

Based on extensive injuries to the old German's head, Doctor Watkins said he believed someone repeatedly struck Schmerer with a blunt instrument. "A hatchit [*sic*] or pick," he said, "...any single one of the injuries...would have produced death." He stated, too, that the body apparently was still warm when it was forced under the rock, because they found it in a "bent position, almost on the hands and knees."

ALL POINTS BULLETIN

Based upon all available evidence, the jurors concluded Owens must have killed Jake so Sheriff Canton sent "Wanted" circulars to lawmen throughout the area, offering a reward for capture of the suspect. His efforts quickly paid off when officers in Miles City, Montana, approximately 180 miles northeast, reported they had picked up Owens and had him in their jail.

On Sunday, May 31, Deputy Sheriff John McDermott went to Miles City to retrieve the young felon. Although he met Owens there for the first time, he recognized him instantly from witnesses' descriptions: "five feet ten inches, with black curly hair, and seemed a happy man." To facilitate the transfer, McDermott brought requisition papers, "but it was not necessary to use them as Owens was willing to come without them." The lawman knew, too, of Owens's reputation as well as the threats the killer faced back in Buffalo. Residents there expressed interest in getting a rope around his neck with or without benefit of a trial. Faced with those prospects, McDermott greeted with relief Miles City Deputy Sheriff W. D. Smith's offer to escort him and the prisoner back to Wyoming.

"Yup, I did it"

Although anxious to learn what Owens had to say about the crime for which he had been charged, McDermott held his curiosity in check until they stepped off the Northern Pacific train at Custer Station. While waiting at the local hotel that afternoon for a stagecoach that would take them back to Sheridan, however, McDermott finally broached the subject: "Did you kill Jake Schmerer?"

"Yup, I did," replied Owens, "but I'll tell you about it later."

Boarding the stage, Owens took a seat facing McDermott and Smith. Like a dog with his nose out the window, looking back towards the dust plumes that curled off the wheels, he seemed more curious about where he had been than focused on where he knew he must go.

Riding through a storm that night brought little rest. The next morning they crossed into Wyoming Territory and reached the Pass Creek Stage Station, where the driver mercifully stopped for breakfast and a change of horses. Although Owens had remained ominously quiet after leaving Custer Station, he suddenly, and without prompting, continued his confession. Whether bothered by his conscience or, more likely, bored with the bumpy, seemingly endless, southbound ride, Owens began to tell his terrible tale somewhere between breakfast and a relief stop at the Forty Mile Stage Station.

He said he arrived at Buffalo in July or August 1884 and hired on to help Jake Schmerer with haying. After about a month, Jake paid him off and he left the area. After kicking around at a number of odd jobs during the next few months, Owens returned. That December, Jake struck a deal with him to go down on Crazy Woman Creek to "kill him some meat." He returned to Schmerer's place about mid-December after cold weather set in and he remained there until early 1885. Again, Jake prevailed on young Owens to return to Crazy Woman to get some more wild game for him. Jake promised grub and ammunition in exchange for any venison Owens brought back. After stocking up with supplies, including poison to kill coyotes, the young hunter went back to the hunting grounds where he dug a cave in which to stay. About three or four weeks later, he returned to Buffalo to trade some coyote skins for additional vittles. Hoping Jake would stake him to some more ammo, Owens went to visit

Schmerer at his cabin. Jake immediately demanded to know whether the young man had killed any deer. Owens assured Jake that he had bagged four or five. Jake said, "I will go right down into town and get my team and go down after them." Owens replied, "Jake, bring me out some cartridges.... If you have got the money I would like for you to get about a hundred if you can."

Jake rushed off to Buffalo where he sold the promised game meat to his old employers McCray and Charley Buell, who planned to feed the venison to patrons of their Occidental Hotel. But, when the German returned to his cabin with only "about 50 or 60 bullets," Owens seethed in silence because he had hardly enough cartridges to pay back the ones he had borrowed from old man Harmon, who lived down on Crazy Woman. The furious Owens decided to teach Schmerer a lesson. With Jake on his saddle horse and Owens and Frank Kelly in a wagon, the three men headed directly for Crazy Woman, where they planned to camp for the evening before retrieving the deer. The following morning Owens snapped the trap on Schmerer by lying that he could not remember where he had cached the carcasses. Although Jake and his companions left the area with little further discussion, Owens learned later from mutual acquaintances that Jake was embarrassed as well as "very hot" because of Owens's trick. In fact, the spiteful old German swore he would blow Owens's brains out if he got the chance.

THE SHOWDOWN

After stopping in Buffalo to buy some groceries and tobacco, Owens started back to his dugout. But his thin gloves simply could not shut out the late afternoon cold, so an hour before sundown on March 25, 1884, he decided to swing by Jake's to warm his hands. Owens described the results of that fatal decision as part of his subsequent District Court testimony:

I went in and spoke to him and said, "How do you do, Jake?" He didn't say how do you do or nothing of the kind. I thought maybe it was just his way. He seemed to have a sulky way. I didn't pay much attention to it. I laid the groceries down on the table and went up to the stove to warm my hands.

It was Jake's habit during the day...he wears a pair of heavy shoes and at night he has a pair of low slippers to slip on around the house. He had been out somewhere doing up his evening work, I think. He was sitting on the bed, I believe, when I came in. He looked kind of sour. I thought maybe the man was drunk or something. Didn't pay much attention to him.

He pulled off his shoes, put on his slippers and when he got them on, I had got my hands over the stove and a little warm by that time. He says, "What did you lie about those deer for?"

"I just done that for a joke, Jake. I didn't mean any harm by that."

"Yes, you damned son of a bitch. I am going to blow your bastard brains out for it."

"There ain't any use in that."

At the same time, he was saying this he was getting up and reaching for his gun [hanging on the wall above his bed]. *I says, "I had rather pay you for the*

Although the main street of Buffalo, Wyoming (circa 1880), is said to follow an old bison trail, a lottery pro-duced the town's name. Five early residents, who each put a name on a slip of paper, dropped their entries in a hat. The winner, "Buffalo," was put in by Alvin J. McCray, a native of Buffalo, New York. The first county fair in the state took place in Buffalo in 1887, the year following John Owen's execution. (Courtesy Wyoming Division of Cultural Resources)

trouble of coming down there or give you a month's work than have any trouble about it. You might as well put the gun up."

"No, I won't do any such thing. I'll blow your brains out if it is the last thing I ever do."

Owens said he begged Jake to put the gun down as the furious German slipped a round into the breech block. All the while, Jake's cursing continued. Nothing would pacify the old man. Owens continued:

It was only a couple of steps from where I was standing to where he was. I stepped up to take the gun away from him. He got it up and hit me over the head with it and staggered me back a little and came up again.

I threw up both hands to catch the gun. He raised the gun to make another lick at me and hit me in the hand and I caught it. I tried to twist it out of his hands. Finally I got it away from him and he began to kick me in the shins when I was trying to take it away from him.

After I got it away from him, there was a chair stood by the end of the table without any back, just the bottom of the chair. He picked the chair up.

First though, when I took the gun away from him, I threw the breech block open and threw the cartridge out on the floor. He picked the chair up and hit me on the shoulder and that numbed my arm a little. I let go [with] my left hand, dropped the gun out and went for the chair. I threw up my hands to catch the chair. He hit me on the elbow that numbed my left arm so I could not use it, but I caught the chair with my right hand and kept him from striking me with it for awhile.

Right behind the stove he kept a wood pail.... I looked around there and saw a piece of board...maybe an inch or an inch and a quarter thick and four or five wide. It was standing right in the corner behind the stove, the same corner [as] the stove.... By that time with scuffling we got up behind the stove. I left the chair and went for the board.

He hit me and knocked me down behind the stove [where] he could not hit me with the chair, so I got hold of the piece of board anyway, raised up and got out when he had the chair up waiting for me. I reached up and grabbed the chair as he struck at me. I struck at him with this piece of board, passed the board over the chair, didn't hit the man at all and broke the board over the chair just as he struck at me. Then we went scuffling for the chair. I tried to take it away from him and went to throw it at him. He dodged in under me and got to the stove where I dropped the gun. I hit the wall with the chair. He reached down and picked up the gun and the cartridge lying near the gun and went to loading the gun again.

I was looking around me to find something to defend myself with, whatever it might be, saw the hatchet lying within two or three feet, stopped and got it. By that time, he had the gun loaded, but didn't have the breech block down on the cartridge in the gun. I commenced striking at him with this hatchet. How many times, I don't know, or where I don't know, but I must have hit him in two or three places.

When asked why Jake's "head was so stove in," Owens said simply, "Well, you know how it is when a man's excited; he don't know when to quit."

THE PLAID TOMBSTONE

Exhausted by the brutal battle which, according to Owens, lasted roughly ten to fifteen minutes, he tried to rest and win back his wits. Later, he said he searched the cabin and the body for money. Finding none, he tied a blue jumper and coat around Jake's head with a quarter-inch cotton clothesline, "to keep the blood off." Then he carried Jake's body to the hills to bury him. Soon tiring, he returned for one of Jake's horses over which he draped the corpse. Proceeding on down a canyon, he finally found a spot where runoff water had eroded soil from under a rock outcropping. After covering the body with small rocks, he returned to the cabin. Exhausted, he collapsed on the bed where he spent the rest of that fitful night.

Very early the next morn, he arose to clean the gore off the floor and walls before walking into town where he arrived an hour or two after sun-up. Although he said he planned to turn himself in to the authorities, second thoughts put him on a path to escape. As soon as the drugstore opened, he redeemed a pistol he had pawned there previously. From there he went back to Jake's place to get the horses he realized would be helpful to his flight. Stopping by Madden's, Owens stayed until mid-afternoon before returning to Jake's corral for the three horses. Madden's unexpected appearance and stay for hotcakes, however, delayed the young man's plans until after dinner. Swapping his gum boots for Jake's leather ones, Owens packed his victim's grub, weapons, and bedding on two of the horses before riding the third mount on a trail that took him across

Clear Creek between town and Fort McKinney. At that point, he said he:

> ...*went over the country north along the foot hills until it came daytime, traveled by night, crossed the Big Horn below Fort Custer a little way, about a half a mile and then followed the old telegraph line through to Billings* [Montana]. *Stopped in or about Billings somewhere, traded the three horses off...for one pony,* [later] *sold the pony for $40.00.*

In Billings, he replaced Jake's boots with another pair.

So ended Owens's confession. Stunned by what they heard, the lawmen silently rocked and bounced in the southbound coach as they tried unsuccessfully to make sense out of Owens's droning, unemotional disclosure.

RETURN TO BUFFALO

When the stage finally reached the Wolf Creek Station, a note from Sheriff Canton awaited McDermott. The sheriff advised his deputy that he would meet him at Sheridan and escort him and his prisoner back to Buffalo so Smith could return to Miles City.

After reuniting, Sheriff Canton and Deputy McDermott continued to Buffalo arriving there on Sunday evening, June 7, with their prisoner in tow. When Owens appeared at his preliminary hearing the following day, he wasted no time in waiving examination and pleading "Not guilty." It was then back to jail for the young felon to await trial in the district court.

The subsequent trial, that lasted only three days, ended on Friday, July 10. With Charles H. Burritt and H.S. Elliott serving as prosecuting attorneys, the jury quickly found Owens "guilty of murder in the first degree." Shortly thereafter, Second Judicial District Court Judge Jacob B. Blair pronounced the death sentence. The local newsmen covering the sentencing expressed amazement at Owens's demeanor. "There was not even at this time a visible sign of any change in Owens," they reported, "and he returned to his cell in as jovial mood as…he was before his trial commenced." J.D. Hinkle, the defense attorney, later obtained a stay of execution for his client thus halting, for a time at least, Owens's court-ordered execution. The Wyoming Territorial Supreme Court, however, upheld that judgment and set March 5, 1885, as the date Owens would be hanged.

ESCAPE ATTEMPTS THWARTED

In the meantime, as Owens sat in his small cell—a cage of strap-iron—contemplating his past, the condemned man seemed to sense that unless he took action into his own hands, there would be no future. Certainly the justice system did not seem to offer much hope. He faced either a noose or, at best, a very long stay in this jail where his creature comforts consisted mainly of a couple of blankets and a mattress on the floor. He also had a small wooden table, a candle, and a can with water that served as a toilet.

What to do? If necessity is the mother of invention, then Owens's desperation surely must have stepped forward to sire the following novel plan for escape. He asked Sheriff Canton for writing paper, some pens, and ink. As the days wore on, the convict periodically asked for additional nibs. One day when the sheriff prepared to open the door to give a meal to

Jacob B. Blair, appointed to the Wyoming Supreme Court on February 14, 1876, by President Ulysses S. Grant, served as an Associate Justice of that judicial body until April 23, 1888. During that time, while also judge of the Second Judicial District Court, he presided over both the 1884 murder trial of George Cooke in Laramie, Wyoming, and that of John Owens in 1885 at Buffalo, Wyoming. (Courtesy Wyoming Division of Cultural Resources)

Owens, another inmate named "Big Belly," a Crow Indian, warned the sheriff that "He [Owens] heap fixum killee you." Once alerted, Canton investigated and found Owens had filed through the half-inch rivets on his leg irons and planned to beat the lawman unconscious with the chains before escaping. Although the authorities failed at that time to discover how Owens had cut the rivets off his shackles, a friend of the prisoner disclosed the secret years later:

> He would take one of those steel nibs and hold it over the candle until it was red hot and straighten it out flat. Then he would make small nicks by rubbing it against the sharp edges of his leg shackle. He would then reheat the nib, temper it in urine and when it wore out he would dispose of it in the sanitary bucket.

With time rapidly running out, Owens once more tried to flee. This time he joined another inmate named John Carson, who had been arrested for "petit larceny." On Sunday evening, November 29, Owens again failed as he tried to escape with the aid of Leo Lambrigger, a trustee, guilty of "dogging" or running cattle with dogs. It seems Lambrigger, because of the minor nature of his crime, was allowed more freedom than the other men and had spent that afternoon in the corridor of the jail. For some unknown reason—perhaps for sheer cussedness—he unfastened the lever that held the cell doors shut. Fortuitously, as Sheriff Canton locked up for the day, he checked the cells and discovered Owens and Carson missing. When Lambrigger denied knowing anything about his compatriots' whereabouts, Big Belly signalled to the lawman that the fugitives were hidden in an area above one of the cage-like cells.

When Canton crawled up into the rather narrow area, he found the jailbirds crouched in about a foot of water inside a tank with its lid closed. After being ordered out of hiding, Owens made a move as if he intended to resist. Canton immediately answered the threat by clubbing the prisoner unconscious with his six-shooter. With a second pistol in his other hand, Canton held Carson at bay. After the prisoners begged the officer to spare their lives, the lawman had no further trouble getting them back into their cells.

Apparently the lesson did not stick. About one month later, Owens tried to carve his way out of his cell with the steel shank from a boot or shoe. When Sheriff Canton made a precautionary search of Owens's cage on November 30, he found his prisoner had cut a hole large enough to make possible an escape under the wall. In the lining of Owens's coat collar, the lawman also found a second metal plate that had been nicked into a saw-like blade.

THE SENTENCE WAS JUSTIFIED

As he neared the end of his rope—literally as well as figuratively—Owens finally admitted to a *Buffalo Sentinel* reporter that his "Bill Booth" moniker was fictitious. He also shared information regarding his pre-Buffalo days. Owens explained that he had been born at Tippeecanoe in Miami County, Ohio, in 1862. Until the age of seventeen, he lived at home where he worked on his father's farm. After the death of his mother, he went to Illinois where shortly after his arrival he married. His wife, unfortunately, died of smallpox only two days after giving birth to a child who, several days later, also succumbed.

Behind this Johnson County Courthouse in Buffalo, Wyoming, circa 1884, condemned John Owens followed his old, Jewish friend, Abe Abrahams, into the jailyard. At Owens's request, Abrahams held a large brass crucifix above his head as he led the murderer up the thirteen steps of the gallows and to the noose. (Courtesy Wyoming Division of Cultural Resources)

Owens drifted westward, first to Kansas, then into the Indian Territory and from there into Texas. Later he went to Colorado before moving into the Wyoming Territory in 1884.

He also admitted to the reporter that he planned Jake's murder a month prior to the time it occurred. He committed the crime, he admitted, after "having had some difficulty with Schmerer over a five dollar transaction." Apparently clearing his conscience, the condemned man reportedly rested well that night.

THE LAST DAY OF THE REST OF HIS BRIEF LIFE

Fresh from a haircut and shave by Joe Sharp, the town barber, the night before, Owens arose at 7:30 A.M. on the last day of his life: March 5, 1886. Following breakfast, Sheriff Canton joined him in the cell to read the death warrant. A brief time later, blacksmith Ole Hogerson entered with a hammer, cold chisel, and square chunk of iron to cut the rivets, freeing the shackles from Owens's legs.

Slightly less than two-and-a-half hours later, the sheriff and his deputies escorted the prisoner into the jail yard behind the courthouse. Dressed in a new black suit, white shirt, white socks, and a pair of black slippers, he followed his old Jewish friend Abe Abrahams, who, at Owens's request, held a large brass crucifix above his friend's head as he led Owens to the gallows and up the thirteen steps to the noose. When asked if he had any last statement, Owens inquired, "What time is it?" When told it was 11 A.M., he said, "I wish you'd hurry up. I want to get to hell in time for dinner."

Satan served the first course precisely twelve minutes later.

SOURCES CITED

Research for this story was complicated by the fact that, unlike most county criminal case documents, those from Johnson County are not readily available at the Wyoming State Archives. Fortunately, however, the Wyoming Supreme Court File #2-30 contains copies of the most important criminal case files regarding Owens's murder of Jake Schmerer.

Other primary sources of value included vintage coverage of the event by the *Daily Sun* and *Democratic Leader* (Cheyenne, Wyoming), the *Big Horn Sentinel* (Big Horn, Wyoming), and the *Buffalo Bulletin* (Buffalo, Wyoming) newspapers.

Several secondary references that offer insight to the characters involved are *Buffalo's First Century*, compiled in 1984 by the Buffalo Centennial Book Committee (Buffalo, Wyoming), plus articles in the *Annals of Wyoming* by Howard B. Lott and Burton S. Hill, respectively entitled, "The Old Occidental" (April, 1955, Vol. 27, No. 11) and "Buffalo–Ancient Cow Town: A Wyoming Saga" (October, 1963, Vol. 35, No. 2).

Lastly, for those who may be curious about Owen and his Johnson County Jail cell mates, the *Johnson County Sheriff's Record Book* (October 1881-September 10, 1912) will be of special interest.

Ben Carter

Badman From Bitter Creek

IT WAS SENSELESS. It was mean. It was murder. And there was only one person to blame: "Big Ben" Carter, the self-proclaimed "Badman from Bitter Creek."

Born in 1850 to German parents in Horton County, Texas, Benjamin F. Carter—if, indeed, that was his name—was a bully of the worst sort. He was six-foot, one-inch, 210 pounds, broad-shouldered, bull-necked with an attitude and temper to match. He also was a loud-mouthed coward, surly and vile. To make matters worse, the florid-faced brute usually carried a small arsenal and bought his courage by the bottle.

The blond badman arrived in Wyoming about 1877 or 1878, fresh from service with the infamous Olive gang, and seemed more than a little anxious to prove himself worthy

135

Benjamin F. Carter bullied a young cowboy during a roundup in the northwestern part of Carbon County before shooting him to death one night in their tent. After failing an attempt to escape the Carbon County jail, the "Badman from Bitter Creek" hanged for that homicide on October 6, 1888, in Rawlins, Wyoming. (Sketch by Eileen Hayes Skibo)

of that band's rancid reputation. Giving the devil his due though, he proved himself to be a damned good cowpunch-er, having worked cattle "since he was old enough to strad-dle a horse." He also drove the old Texas Trail through Salina and Abilene in Kansas, on to Ogallala, Nebraska, and to Ellsworth in the Dakota Territory so many times that few could claim more experience with a herd.

During his first several years in Wyoming, he worked for some of the most successful cattlemen in the Territory including Bob Stafford, Jim Ferris, and J. Rosenfield. His first job as foreman came when he hired on with the Charles Herbertz Land and Cattle Company that ranged its stock on the Laramie Plains. Even then he looked for trouble when it didn't find him first. On one occasion, he and nasty "Big" Nadler brutally beat a Laramie City night watchman. When N.K. Boswell, the Albany County Sheriff, learned of the incident, he left his bed to find the hooligans in a local saloon, drinking and congratulating themselves on their exploits. Boswell quickly cowed the bullies with his six-shooter and marched them off to jail.

Carter remained "top hand" on the spread for the next five-and-a-half years, even after Herbertz sold his cattle company to the Dole brothers. Carter subsequently went to work at the Hub and Spoke ranch owned by Ed C. Johnson and Tom Sun.

THE BULLY BUTCHERS THE BOY

He worked well there, too, as long as he stayed away from the "bug juice." Unfortunately, according to Ben's own account, he "had been drinking for nearly a week" before that fateful day of October 4, 1886. "We left the Hub and Spoke ranch with the wagon and riders to start on the beef round-up on the Sweetwater," Carter related. "I went by Jim Averell's road ranch," he said, "and drank whisky there."

By the time Carter caught up with the roundup about nine that evening, still toting his quart bottle of "Dutch Courage," the rest of the crew already had set up camp on Sand Creek, about thirty miles northeast of Rawlins and six miles from Ferris. Included in the group was a "small and very quiet" cowboy about seventeen years old named James Jeffries. Although Carter admitted he never had any problems with Jim, the belligerent Ben's cold, light blue eyes turned dark as a summer prairie storm fired by the liquor's lightning as soon as he saw the lad. Carter nearly always spoiled for a fight, especially with someone younger and smaller. Jim, a "slip of a boy," fit that description to a tee.

Young Jeffries came to Wyoming in 1882 from his home in Missouri and went to work for the W.H. Holliday company. He only joined the Johnson and Sun outfit about two weeks before this confrontation with Carter.

No sooner had Badman dismounted than he lit into Jim accusing him of being a "damned spotter" [a spy] for the Stockgrowers' Association. When Jeffries indignantly denied that charge, Carter repeated the assertion. While holding Jim at bay with his Colt .45, the bully kicked the youth and slapped his face two or three times, all the while cursing the kid and his pedigree. Kinney Debardeben and Walter Forrest, two other cowboys with the roundup, might have helped—should have helped—but they knew only too well that "Carter the drunk" made "Carter the bully" look like a

Albany County Sheriff N. K. Boswell (circa 1885) once arrested and briefly jailed Ben Carter for brutally beating a Laramie City night watchman. Carter suffered the permanent punishment, however, after murdering fellow wrangler Jim Jeffries while they herded cows on Sand Creek about thirty miles northeast of Rawlins, Wyoming. (Courtesy Wyoming Division of Cultural Resources)

pansy. Better leave him alone, they reasoned, until he sobered up. If the truth was known, they probably feared Carter almost as much as the more vulnerable Jeffries.

Temporarily sated, Carter went into the sleeping tent, but soon he was back outside, ordering Jim to pack up and leave the camp the next morning. When Jeffries refused, more blows and abuse followed. Trying to avoid a fight, or worse, Jim swallowed his pride and finally retired to the tent. Faced with an early morning start, Debardeben, Forrest, and Carter soon joined the young cowhand. As Carter recalled:

We finally went to bed, sleeping in the tent. When I was in my blankets someone made a remark about shooting a hole in the roof of the tent.

I had my pistol under my pillow. I got it out, a Colt's [sic] .45, and shot twice through the top of the tent and then laid it down by the bed. A short time after that I picked it up to try another shot on the roof. The notches of the "dog" which holds the hammer up when raised had been filed, so the hammer wouldn't stay cocked, and when I raised the gun up it was prematurely discharged.

Of the six beds in the tent that night, three lined the north wall, facing east, to the left of the door-fly. Carter's cot dominated the middle. Two more hugged the south wall with Jim's bed in the southeast corner.

As I raised the gun I cocked it and it went off, the ball striking Jeffries in the head. After this last shot I had laid down again and in about a minute one of the boys said: "You have shot Jeffries."

Debardeben said, "Ben, I suppose you're satisfied now; you've killed him." "I guess not," slurred Carter. Only after

Badman got out of bed and struck a match did others in the tent realize the terrible truth. The slug, which hit Jeffries about two inches above the left eye, passed through his head. He remained unconscious and died nine hours later.

SUNUP AT THE HUB AND SPOKE

Carter immediately pulled on his clothes and ordered Forrest to pull a good mount out of the herd so he could escape. When Forrest refused, Carter rushed outside where he saddled a horse before racing off alone into the night.

In the meantime, the other cowboys made Jeffries as comfortable as possible before Debardeben and Forrest rode to the camp of their foreman, "Hi" Bernard. Rheumatic and unable to ride, their boss sent the two men off "to warn the neighboring ranchmen to be on the lookout for the safety of their horses and for the fleeing Carter." The men went straight to the Hub and Spoke to tell Tom Sun what happened. From there, they rode on to John and Tom Durbin's Lazy UT "Buzzard" ranch.

At nearly the same time, Carter searched to find another mount. Unable to find one, he headed for Sun's, where he arrived shortly after the departure of Debardeben and Forrest, about daylight on October 5. Without telling what had happened, he simply asked his boss for a fresh horse, but Sun, already aware of the crime, quickly disarmed him. A short time later, Debardeben and Forrest returned with the Durbin Brothers' foreman, Tom Lowe.

After the group had some breakfast, Sun turned Carter over to Lowe, and asked Debardeben and Forrest to escort the foreman and his prisoner into Rawlins. Sun followed in his wagon a few hours later with what was left of the once happy and genial Jeffries.

On the way into town, Carter "fell" from his horse and feigned injury, but his guards simply drew their guns and ordered him to remount. Carter's scheme seemed to be to lure his captors out of their saddles so that he could subdue the smaller men and escape on their fresher horses. After being on the trail continuously for more than nineteen hours, they finally arrived at the sheriff's office in Rawlins. There they turned their prisoner over to Deputy Sheriff Adams at about eight that night.

The following morning—Tuesday, October 6—the Carbon County Justice of the Peace and Coroner George W. Durant summoned a jury to his office to conduct the inquest. At the end of that day-long investigation, the jury concluded, "...James Jeffries came to his death by a pistol being in the hands of Benjamin F. Carter, a killing ruled 'wilful, malicious and unlawful murder.'"

THE LEGAL PROCESS

Exactly one week later, Carter had a preliminary hearing before Justice Durant. He contended he could not get a fair trial because the newspapers had so inflamed public opinion about his case. He also said he lacked the money to properly defend himself, so Homer Merrell was assigned by the court to serve as the defense attorney. Merrell immediately gained a continuance until the next regular term of the District Court of the Second Judicial District.

With the trial postponed until the following May (1887), Carter had time, with financial support from his family in

Texas, to hire his own defense attorneys, G. Carl Smith of Rawlins and John Cochran Thompson of Cheyenne.

On May 21, 1887, with as many as fifty ladies present at one time in the Carbon County Court, testimony ended in the early afternoon; however, arguments continued until 9 P.M. when Judge Samuel Corn charged the jury before they retired to consider the evidence. Less than three hours later, the jurors returned with their verdict: "Guilty of murder in the first degree." The prosecutor J.R. Dixon prevailed as the judge sentenced Carter to be hanged the coming July 8.

As people in the gallery commended the jury for the verdict, a gentleman from a neighboring county observed ironically, "You people seem determined to hang your murderers and other bad people while you commend your official thieves [politicians]. You are a peculiar people."

After the first sentence, the judge granted a stay of proceeding so that the Wyoming Territory's Supreme Court might rule upon the case. When the lower court's finding was sustained, Judge Corn resentenced Carter to be hanged that August. But the execution again was delayed as Governor Thomas Moonlight granted a respite of sixty-three days so that the Court might consider the defense lawyers' application for a new trial. When it was refused, Carter's attorneys applied for a reversal of judgment on what they claimed were legal technicalities connected with the jury selection. Unfortunately for Carter, the Court refused to disturb the lower court's decision, and the Badman again found himself staring at the noose.

With nearly every effort made to save him from the death penalty, Carter abandoned hope as reports emerged that he felt "very much depressed and broken down."

Under the leadership of Governor Thomas Moonlight, Wyoming Territory's chief executive from January 24, 1887 until April 9, 1889, the legislature initiated a law requiring a coroner's inquest be conducted "upon the dead bodies of such persons only as are supposed to have died by unlawful means, or the cause of whose death is unknown." Governor Moonlight also granted the condemned Ben Carter a respite pending the defense lawyers' application for a new trial. (Courtesy Wyoming Division of Cultural Resources)

Despite what many considered an inordinately patient court as well as exhaustive efforts by his counsels to thwart justice, Carter continued daily to complain *ad nauseam* via the *Daily Boomerang*:

I know I did not have a fair trial. Anybody would know that. If I had intended to kill Jeffries I would not have ridden into camp and there turned my horse loose, undressed and gone to bed. Of course, I know the boys said I had threatened to kill him, but I don't remember anything about that. I had been drinking, but would have remembered that as well as the things I have told you about if I had said it.

I tried to get a change of venue, and I think now if I had succeeded I would never have been convicted of this charge. The prejudice of the people convicted me. A remark had been made by one of the jurors, who was on the regular panel, to other jurymen, but who did not serve in my case, coming up on the train from Carbon, that "if we do not hang Carter, we had better not return to Carbon." Even here in Rawlins men were offering to bet that I would be convicted of murder before any evidence had been offered in my case.

ATTEMPTED ESCAPE

During the first week of July 1887, a trustee named Lacy smuggled a pistol and a saw made from corset steel to Carter in the jail. Fearing he might be caught with the weapon, Carter slipped the six-shooter to a prisoner named McClellan, but authorities discovered the contraband, thwarting the escape. To prevent another attempted flight, the lawman fastened an eight-foot-long chain, with an iron bracelet, around Carter's left ankle, and secured the other end to the iron grating surrounding the cells. "I have worn this chain sixteen months and twenty-one days, and it may not seem much," he complained, "but it is tiresome to drag around."

Carter marked his remaining days by a few events that broke the monotony. He was baptized by his spiritual adviser Reverend R.E.G. Huntington. Then, on the Sunday, October 21, before his execution, he took communion in his cell. When Deputy Sheriff L.C. Kelley was assigned day and night to serve as "death watch" for the Badman-no-more, Carter asked, "What did they hire you for?" Kelley replied, "Just to look at you and keep you company." Laughing at what he apparently considered an absurdity, Carter said, "I think just to wait on me [is not enough] so you had better get me a drink of water." Kelley good-naturedly complied.

During his last week, Carter again showed deep despair. His appetite failed, and he found it almost impossible to sleep. A *Daily Boomerang* reporter observed:

His air of bravado entirely disappeared and the expression of his face was haggard in the extreme. When anyone approached his cell he seemed startled and had a hunted look that almost compelled sympathy for his unfortunate position.

Despite that fit of melancholy, a *Carbon County Journal* newsman, who visited Carter in his cell the night before his execution, found him "cheerful and lively as could be expected under the circumstances." The reporter discovered, in the meantime, that although Carter lacked a formal education, he had learned to speak "Mexican" as well as the German language. Also, as the subject of conversation drifted around to card playing, the prisoner expressed his fondness of Whist and Casino. He claimed he had played 350 games with one of the inmates and won 174 of them.

As he sat eating his last supper of ham, eggs, potatoes, and coffee, Carter told the reporter on the outside of the iron grating that he had been in jail two years and twenty-one days. "It is pretty hard and rocky," he said. He also shared with the newsman that he would welcome a finish to the affair. He was "ready," he said, "and had closed all of his business now on this side of the range." The finality of that remark signaled an end to the interview. But, as the reporter prepared to leave, Carter thoughtfully handed him a bunch of cigars through the grating. He had more than he could use, he said.

Later that night, after his visitors had gone, Carter shaved his wide, square jaws and removed the familiar, short, sandy moustache before going to bed. The night seemed interminable as he slept uncomfortably for only two hours. During most of that long, last night, the doomed man sat quietly with his forehead cupped in his hands as if deep in thought. A cigarette rarely left his lips. Occasionally he perused a prayer book and even sang a few lines of "Nearer My God to Thee" as his heavy voice echoed off the bare, stone walls.

THROUGH THE WINDOW AND INTO HELL

Finally the fateful October 26 arrived: the last day of his life. Resigned to his fate, he arose and had a "hearty breakfast" before Reverend Huntington joined him at 8:40 for an hour of religious devotions. To show his appreciation, Carter said, "You have done for me more than any other man ever did and more than I believed it possible for any man to do." He then embraced the minister and gave him a silver medallion the size of a dollar coin. "Benjamin" was engraved on one side of the polished surface and on the reverse side were the date, thirteen stars, and the likeness of "Liberty." An hour later, twenty-three acquaintances filed through the outer corridor to bid Carter farewell. He grasped their hands as they passed his cell and, with lips trembling, bid each a "goodbye."

The visitors gone, Carter walked up and down the inner aisle of the jail with his shackles clanging at every step. At 9:50 A.M., Carbon County Physician Ricketts and Sheriff High visited him and told him the execution would take place within ten minutes. After being given a shot of whisky to help calm his nerves, the prisoner asked that his time be extended an hour, a promise made, but broken. Carter had no means of knowing the time and failed to notice the breach of faith.

Not wanting to meet his fate in common work boots, Carter asked for a pair of carpet slippers before leaving his cell. The size "eights" that he received were too big, but he surmised he probably "wouldn't loose [sic] them".

Although seemingly pleased the end was here, he expressed disappointment with the blustery weather. The raw stiff breeze and snow flurries filled the air as fewer than one hundred persons braved the weather to congregate near the courthouse in hopes of glimpsing the victim and his tug of war with the noose. Fewer still stood within the "privileged" area near the gallows. Although the law entitled

Reverend R.E.G. Huntington, spiritual adviser to murderer Ben Carter during his imprisonment in the Carbon County jail, baptized the "Badman from Bitter Creek" prior to his execution on October 26, 1890. The holy man, to whom Carter bequeathed his body, carried out a simple burial service that afternoon. At the county's expense he planted Carter in the Rawlins Cemetery. (Courtesy Wyoming Division of Cultural Resources)

Carter to invite six relatives and/or friends to witness his death, he chose only his barber, Ernest Sundin, to attend. Newsmen, other than several Carbon County reporters especially admitted, could only vie for a peek with the rest of the crowd through the cracks in the eighteen-foot high outer board wall that screened the gallows area.

At 10:30 A.M., Sheriff High entered the jail as a procession formed at the door of the building. Deputies immediately brought Carter out into the corridor of the courthouse and led him through the sheriff's apartment. Reverend Huntington followed the prisoner and his guards as they walked quickly through the hushed onlookers. They exited the building by stepping through an open window onto the scaffold erected against the east wall of the courthouse. After testing the snow-covered trap door's strength with his foot, Carter concluded that although the structure was firm, its surface was "slippery."

Standing on the trap, he brought his heels together so Deputy Thomas Hanks could firmly bind his ankles and thighs with leather straps. Hanks also wrapped another thong around Carter's arms and chest before manacling his hands behind his back. Just before Deputy Kelly adjusted the knot of the noose, Carter said in a clear, firm voice, "Sheriff High, I thank you for your kind treatment of me." Then, turning halfway around, the doomed man saw Doctor Osborne and Doctor Ricketts standing beneath the platform where, after the trap sprung, they prepared to take his pulse and determine the time of death. Laughing, he said, "Goodbye, Doc. I hope to see you all again." The physician replied, "Goodbye, Ben. I hope so." Then the noose of five-eights-inch, soap-lubricated hemp was snugged around his neck. When asked if it was too tight, Carter said, "No, draw it tighter" before Deputy Kelley pulled the glossy black, silk cap over the Badman's balding head. Within a moment, following a prearranged signal, Sheriff High, concealed in a nearby sentry box, cut the cord that held the trap in place. At precisely 10:37, Carter dropped through four feet of space and the rope snapped tight with a quick jerk.

Only four minutes later, the doctors pronounced him dead before having him cut down and carried into the southeast corner of the jail where they placed his body on a cooling board. As spectators passed to view the corpse, each received a bit of the hanging rope, cut into souvenirs by the presiding officials.

Reverend Huntington, to whom Carter had bequeathed his body, carried out a simple burial service that afternoon at the county's expense, before permanently planting his charge in the Rawlins Cemetery.

SOURCES CITED

In addition to Carbon County Criminal Case File #180 which provided the most detailed and substantive research documentation about this case, several newspapers of that time contain specifics about Carter, his past, his crime, plus the events surrounding his imprisonment and execution. Most specifically, the *Carbon County Journal* and *Wyoming Tribune* (Cheyenne, Wyoming) as well as the *Boomerang* (Laramie, Wyoming), and the *Cheyenne Daily Leader* (Cheyenne, Wyoming) provide the most colorful details without which this story would not be nearly so interesting. The reader may find the July 6, 1888, edition of the *Carbon County Journal* of special interest; a letter to the editor from Carter appears on page 3.

George Black

Fingered by the Fire

ALTHOUGH A NEWCOMER to the Pole Mountain area, Mary Backus had no fear of losing her way on horseback while searching the surrounding glens and glades for wild berries. A compass of natural landmarks helped her keep her bearings. The most insignificant of those was Eagle Rock. Like a giant child's great grey blocks heaped high in the center of a green and tan patched carpet, the volcanic mass stood out clearly just about a half mile to the southwest. Greentop Mountain, too, loomed against the blue Wyoming sky. And on the horizon, nearly three miles away beneath the late afternoon sun, prominent Pilot Hill watched over Laramie City far to the west.

So even though she and her parents had only moved there a few days earlier, the sixteen-year-old girl confidently left the main trail that August 6, 1889, to shortcut the two mile trek northwest to her home. Still that decision nagged her. There had been so much talk by her folks and others concerning the recent disappearance of "Ol' Bob" Burnett that she could not help but keep her eyes peeled as she rode along. An uncertainty nagged her, because she had never met the old man who lived over on Pole Creek. As she entered a remote canyon surrounded by timber, she spied an odd pile of ashes at the end of a partially burned seventy-foot log. Its tip rested in the middle of a bare burned spot some eight feet in diameter. Although she continued on, the sight so intrigued her that she returned for a closer look. She still did not dismount, but when she saw bone fragments that looked suspiciously like fingers, she quickly spurred her horse home to tell her mother, Mattie Pullman, what she believed she had found. A meeting of family members followed during which they decided that Mattie and Mary should go to the mystery site. Fearing someone might be watching the area, they agreed it would be safer if Mattie's deaf husband, Charles, accompanied them.

The next morning Mary led her parents back to the secluded site where they found bones and miscellaneous bits of waste which they scraped from the spent fire into two quart pails: one tin and one wood. Later that day Charles, his "nervous somewhat excited" wife, and her daughter took the debris and rode west to Laramie, where they delivered it to Herman V.S. Groesbeck, the Albany County Attorney. Groesbeck immediately called Doctor John W. Harris and an associate to his office, where they carefully sifted "a handful of bones" from the mixed matter. The physicians had no difficulty identifying "two or three phalanges—the finger bones." They also found some teeth, portions of a skull, and a rib. There were rivets, too, like those used to reinforce a man's canvas overalls, plus hobnails from work shoes. And bits of bailing wire. Most significantly, they located a button in the debris that bore the stamp of "T.T. Smith & Co.," an Omaha firm. Only J.S. Watkins' store in Laramie sold such Nebraska-made goods.

Strange! The missing Robert Burnett always wore overalls... and he always purchased them from Watkins.

THE ECCENTRIC "OL' TANGLEFOOT"

Of those familiar with "Ol' Tanglefoot" Burnett, most believed him to be a crazy old coot. The newspapers charitably called the sixty-year-old man "eccentric."

Burnett had been a prosperous farmer when he lived near Meridian, Missouri, during the Civil War. However, he lost everything when he sold his herd of 144 mules to the rebel forces for what proved to be worthless Confederate money. That financial reversal and the subsequent death of his wife caused him to turn westward. By the time he arrived in the Wyoming Territory in 1875, Tanglefoot's peculiarities only seemed to grow more pronounced. He wore gunny sacks tied or wired around his feet even through the heat of summer. The peculiar gait resulting from the use of that awkward footwear provided his nickname. He also ate only with his hands and dumped the scraps on the cabin floor where he slept. And if that weren't enough, he had not been known to shake hands with a bar of soap since he moved into the area some fourteen years earlier. Not that his peculiar ways any longer mattered. It seemed certain, based upon preliminary findings, that he had been dead for about nine weeks when the young mountain girl stumbled—almost literally—across his burned bones.

After leaving their frightful find with Groesbeck, the Pullmans and daughter Mary grew fearful that, once word spread about their visit to town, it would be unsafe for them to return to their ranch. They had seen someone who definitely did not resemble Ol' Bob's description guarding Burnett's cabin with a rifle. Clearly, they feared for their lives and decided to stay at least that night in town.

Early the following day, Sheriff Charles Yund and attorney Groesbeck went out to where the bones had been recovered to see what additional light they could shed on the subject. After talking to other settlers in the area and learning that local drifter George Black had moved into Burnett's shack shortly after the old man turned up missing, they went to the isolated site described by Mary and her mother. They found additional body parts plus a bit of burned gunnysack. A jury convened that Friday afternoon to investigate the case.

During the next five days, thirty to forty witnesses testified about the crime. The coroner, Dr. J.H. Hayford, the sheriff, members of the jury, and other principals spent one of these days combing through Burnett's unoccupied cabin. In the end, the jurymen unanimously agreed:

> *We are satisfied from expert testimony that they are the bones of a human being, and from the remnants of clothing found with* [sic], *and the size of the bones, that they are the remains of a coarsely clad, adult male.*
>
> *The mysterious recent disappearance of Robert Burnett, in the vicinity of where these bones were found, raises a strong presumption that they are his bones.*

Evidence before the jury of ill feeling, contention, lawsuits and rival claims and interests, together with various threats by George [A.] Black and [his sidekick] Dwight "Roxy" Rockwell, and the fact that the said Black and Rockwell took possession of the ranch and property of said Burnett immediately after his disappearance, and also certain mysterious acts since then on the part of said Black and Rockwell, raise a strong suspicion in the minds of the jury that these remains are the bones of Robert Burnett and that he was feloniously murdered by said George Black and Dwight Rockwell about the last days of May or first days of June, 1889, and that they endeavored to hide their crime by burning the body of said Burnett.

The jury directed "that their most thorough and persistent effort be made by the proper authorities to discover and bring to justice the authors of the crime."

Although no firm evidence implicated George's brother Benjamin, attorney Groesbeck promptly had both men arrested. Following a preliminary hearing on Thursday, August 22, before Justice of the Peace Charles E. Carpenter, authorities returned George to his cell in the Albany County jail for safe keeping, but they released Ben for lack of evidence. In the meantime, the twenty-eight-year-old Rockwell had skipped the country shortly after Burnett's reported disappearance and had not been seen since.

GEORGE A. BLACK AND HIS COHORT IN CRIME

Black, age twenty-seven when he was jailed, had been born in Wayne County, Indiana, on August 24, 1862. At the age of eight, he moved with his parents, three sisters, and two brothers (one of whom was Benjamin) to Ryan County in Missouri, where his father died. His mother subsequently moved to Davis County, Missouri. As a sickly child, he "could not bear up under even the confinement of the school room" so, with no formal education, he never learned to read or write. About 1880, he moved to Laramie, where his health improved, and he engaged in ranching and freighting. He also helped grade and level most of Laramie's streets. There he met and wed Sarah Marker, a fifty-three-year-old widow with six youngsters, who was 25 years older than he. When their marriage failed about four years later, Sarah remained with her children in Laramie while Black moved out on his own and sought consolation by joining the local Baptist church [his mother's faith].

While George awaited his preliminary hearing, a break came in the case against his pal Rockwell. Sheriff Yund learned that a check made payable to and endorsed by Rockwell had been received from North Park in northern Colorado. The sheriff immediately swore out an arrest warrant and deputized J.J. Moore to assist. The two lawmen headed south across the state line on Wednesday, August 21. Soon they located their man at work in a field on George Fletcher's ranch on the Michigan River. Rockwell assumed the two armed men were grouse hunters and showed no particular concern as they rode by. Suddenly they turned back and Yund asked, "This is Dwight Rockwell, I believe." "Yes," he unhesitatingly replied. "Then I have a warrant for your arrest," said Moore, before producing and reading the warrant. Upon hearing the charges against him, Rockwell cried, "My God! Have they rung me in on that thing anyway? I had expected that."

Vindictive George Black put three fatal bullets into the body of "Ol' Tanglefoot" Burnett, a litigious hermit who was killed as he sat cutting seed potatoes in his mountain cabin. Black's crime sent him up the steps of a scaffold built inside the same two-story wooden shed in Laramie City where authorities had hanged George Cooke. (Sketch by Eileen Hayes Skibo)

The well-built prisoner of more than average height (five-foot, ten-inches tall) accompanied the lawmen without either resistance or written authorization by Colorado authorities. Before leaving the area, the sheriff and his deputy learned that Rockwell had arrived at Fletcher's place about a month earlier. He made no attempt to conceal his identity although, at times, those who knew him said he appeared moody and absent-minded. In fact, on one occasion, Mrs. Fletcher asked him what bothered him. He said "he had had trouble before leaving Wyoming, that the trouble had been over land matters and that on account of it a certain person had 'taken a shot' at him."

On the way back to Laramie, Rockwell asked many questions about the Burnett murder case. He wanted to know, for example, what the effect would be if a man turned state's evidence in the forthcoming trial. He added that "he did not propose that any innocent man should suffer on account of Burnett's death," but when questioned he lapsed into a moody silence as black as his hair. Sheriff Yund did learn something of his prisoner's history during that return trip. Rockwell, having attended a New England "common school," was a bit better educated than his friend Black. Born July 11, 1861, in South Windsor, Connecticut, Rockwell's father died eighteen months later leaving his mother, sister, and three brothers nearly destitute. The conditions arising from that family tragedy helped teach him to be self-supporting. Rockwell also attended Sunday School and the Methodist Church. When almost seventeen years old, a year before his mother died, he joined the U.S. Navy as an apprentice sailor. During his subsequent five-year military hitch and later service with the Merchant Marines, he visited Europe, South America, China, and islands throughout the Pacific. Finally in 1887, he moved to Laramie. Never married, young Rockwell drank occasionally, but apparently not to excess. In fact, he enjoyed a fairly trouble-free reputation until he became involved with Black.

Two days after leaving North Park, the sheriff and his deputy arrived in Laramie at 7 P.M. with the dark complected Rockwell in tow. The lawmen had travelled a total of 170 miles while finding, arresting, and returning their man to justice. Upon their return to Laramie, Rockwell promptly requested a meeting with attorney Groesbeck, the prosecutor for this case.

ROXY'S CONFESSION

Later that same night, in the Albany County District Clerk's office of the courthouse, the contrite Rockwell voluntarily told Groesbeck everything he could remember about the terrible crime.

The first step toward the tragedy, according to Rockwell, came when he met Black at the JD Ranch in the Silver Crown mining district. Not until the following April, when they met again in Laramie and they became better acquainted, did Black invite Rockwell to stay with him at his brother Ben's place. While Rockwell stayed there, Black told him that in 1886 he had purchased a cabin and corral from William Fisher, who used the surrounding land to graze sheep. But because the property was on the Fort Sanders timber reservation, it was not possible to obtain a clear title to the property. Black explained he lived there but a short time when the litigious Bob Burnett accused him of cutting some of his hay and brought suit to recover its value. Burnett subsequently won the case. When Black could not pay the prescribed amount, the court awarded Black's buildings, "one or two cows," and some hay land to the old hermit.

When Burnett took over that spread, Black moved to Medicine Bow where he worked for a time in a sawmill. Filled with vengeance, he returned to the Pole Mountain country during the winter of 1888 and moved in with his brother and his family. With Rockwell as a sympathetic compatriot, Black convinced his pal to help him repossess the land he believed rightfully belonged to him. They would share, he said, the profits of whatever they earned that summer from the land. On Monday, May 27, 1889, they went to Laramie, where Rockwell secured a mining claim to the land where Burnett operated his ranch. They also purchased some provisions, cooking utensils, a revolver, and cartridges before returning to Ben's where they practiced with their new pistol.

The following morning, they loaded their provisions into Ben's wagon and drove their team of horses to Burnett's place. Just before reaching the ranch, Rockwell shot at a jack rabbit, bringing "Ol Tanglefoot" out of his cabin. What was he doing there? Rockwell understood from his buddy Black that Burnett would be gone when they arrived. Now what?

Despite Rockwell's dark-eyed pleas to turn back, Black ignored the requests and drove to the property, where he tied their team of horses. After entering the old hermit's shack, Black wasted no time telling Burnett the ranch belonged to him and that Burnett should leave. Burnett, however, adamantly refused to vacate the place saying now that he

Dwight Rockwell, Black's accomplice, helped his cohort-in-crime haul their victim's corpse into the shadow of Eagle Rock, where they tried to hide their crime with a pitch pine fire. Luck helped him escape the noose for that felony only to be shot and killed in Montana two years later. (Sketch by Eileen Hayes Skibo)

owned it, he planned to hold on to it. After arguing for awhile, Black jumped up and began carrying Burnett's things out the door. When Rockwell refused to help, Black returned and took a seat behind Burnett, who continued "cutting up seed potatoes." Suddenly, with no warning, Black drew his revolver with his right hand and fired a slug that lodged eight inches deep in the left side of the old man's back. The mortally wounded Burnett cried out, "Oh, George!" before pitching forward. His arm stretched toward his gun that lay on the nearby table. Black immediately shot him again, this time in the head. As the dying man lay on the floor, Black shot a third bullet into his body. The men then pulled a gunnysack over Burnett's head and used wire to bind a blanket around his body before they tucked the corpse under the bed. In an effort to further hide their crime, Black and Rockwell ripped up the wooden flooring drenched with their victim's blood. As the sun set, they completed tearing out and burning the boards. They then hauled the corpse by wagon several miles to a secluded canyon where they torched a pile of pitch pine logs atop the cadaver. Ominous black shadows danced about the pyre and against the nearby rocks as they rode back to the cabin where they spent the night.

The next morning, they got up early to wash and scrape the blood spots from the wagon before smearing grease on the tarpaulin to mask the dark red stains left by the corpse. After breakfast, they went back to where they had burned old Bob Burnett. The flames had consumed all but the spinal column and some of the larger bones, so they raked these beneath more pitch-rich wood and rekindled the flames before returning to the cabin to patch the floor. That night they again rode back to the fire site, gathered up the most coarse of the remaining bones, and stuck them down a nearby gopher hole before they covered it with a large stone. They then returned to Burnett's shack.

Their work was done. Well done! Nobody would ever know or care, they thought, what had become of the old man. For those who asked, they would be told "Tanglefoot" had gone east to visit his only known relative, a sister. In fact, it might have been a perfect crime except for a girl's curiosity and a co-conspirator's conscience.

THE LEGAL PROCESS

Based upon the facts of his confession, the court indicted Rockwell as an "accessory to murder after the fact." Black, who had been indicted with murder in mid-October, went to the Second District Court grand jury on Saturday, November 2. Although skillfully defended by attorneys J. W. Black and L.D. Pease, their opponent, Prosecuting Attorney Groesbeck more successfully presented the facts to the jury. The following Thursday night, the jury foreman, James Daugherty, announced, "We of the Jury in the above entitled prosecution find the Deph [defendant] George A. Black guilty of the Crime of Murder in the First Degree." The outcome surprised no one. Black "received the verdict with the same insensibility and stoicism which...characterized him throughout the trial." The following morning—Friday, November 16—Judge M.C. Saufley pronounced sentence by ruling that Black be hanged the following January 15.

The only real question left, according to most of those who witnessed the judicial process, dealt not with Black,

Herman V.S. Groesbeck, Albany County Justice of the Peace at the time George Cooke and George Black murdered their two victims, subsequently served as the Chief Justice of the Wyoming Supreme Court from 1890 until 1897. (Courtesy Wyoming Division of Cultural Resources)

but with his co-conspirator. Rockwell's case had not yet been heard.

Within the next few days, George's brother Ben mortgaged all of his property to help raise the $200 needed so that defense attorney William H. Fishback could take Black's case to the Supreme Court of the Wyoming Territory. Maintaining his innocence, and still hopeful that Fishback's efforts would be successful, Black remained not only stoic, but even displayed a bit of good humor. During a reporter's visit to the jail, for example, he heard Black call to Rockwell in another part of the building: "If you are hung before I am, tell them I am coming."

Finally, just three days before his execution, Black received a stay of execution as the case went before the Supreme Court on a bill of exemption. Despite winning that battle, however, he lost the war. Not only did the Court deny his attorney's motion for a new trial while affirming the judgment of the lower court, but Governor Francis E. Warren denied Fishback's pleas as well as calls for clemency from a delegation of clergy and friends.

As Black's imprisonment carried over into February, he continued to maintain his innocence. He also threatened suicide and rejected any offers of spiritual counsel by local clergy, but after Dan B. Davis and Henry Welton arrived at noon on Friday, February 14, to serve as the "death watch," he finally seemed to accept his fate. The "watchers" took turns—twelve hours at a time—and remained on guard.

Finally, Sunday, February 23, arrived as approximately 1,000 persons swarmed about the jail and the twenty-foot square enclosure where, at the east end, stood the scaffold. Like kids at a carnival "cooch" show, they pushed and shoved to find a crack through which to peek inside. Nearly all of them asked to see Black, but after nearly 150 passed by his cell, the condemned man "became irritable and said he wanted to see no more."

THE EXECUTION

At nearly one o'clock in the morning on the last day of his life—February 26, 1890—Black went to bed. Deep sleep would not come as he recalled his brother Ben's tearful visit with him the previous day. Sadly and regrettably he told Ben nothing more than he previously had said to others. He swore that Roxy, not he, fired the fatal shot. Still later, when a guard inquired about Black's tossing and turning in his bunk, the condemned prisoner asked, "You believe I am telling the truth don't you?" Assuring him that he did indeed, Black replied, "I wouldn't for the world die and say that Roxy did the shooting unless he did do it."

That seemingly endless night ended at 6 A.M. when Black arose and bathed before donning a collarless white shirt and slipping into a plain, black suit. Soon after, brother Ben and Father Cumminskey returned to comfort the distraught convict. At about 9:30 A.M., a deputy served Black a breakfast of fried chicken, oysters, crackers, bread, butter, and tea. But he ate very little. A brief time later he shaved before Sheriff Yund came and fulfilled the requirement of reading the dreaded death warrant to him.

Although denying entry to the crowd that thronged the courthouse later that morning, lawmen did admit a handful of special guests such as George's stepdaughter, Mollie [Mary], and her husband, John Wrisinger. They also let his tearful friends Mrs. John Wright and a Mrs. Adams in to visit. Black wept during their meeting. The prisoner seemed touched, too, that Judge Saufley and Reverend H.L. Wriston came to pay their last respects.

Soon after Ben left, Deputy Alexander S. McKay stopped by to explain exactly what would transpire upon the scaffold. "For God's sake, George," said the deputy, "let what you say be the truth. Do not go into the other world

Mr *James Stirling, Ex-Sheriff*
You are hereby invited to be
present at the execution of
GEORGE A. BLACK,
which will take place at the Court
House, in Laramie, Wyoming Terri-
tory, on the 26th day of February,
1890, at the hour of 11 o'clock, A. M.
Not transferable.
CHARLES YUND,
Sheriff Albany County.

*Sheriff Charles Yund took advantage of George Black's murder convic-
tion to invite his friends, fellow lawmen, and other governmental officials to witness the second legal execution in Albany County's history.*
(Courtesy Wyoming Department of Commerce, Division of
Cultural Resources)

with a lie upon your lips." Again bursting into tears, Black
replied:

> *I have told the truth and if I am able I shall do so
> upon the scaffold. I am going up there and shall try to be
> as stout as I can, but I don't know whether I can talk or
> not. The only thing I have to be forgiven for is telling a
> lie in the beginning to save Roxy.*

The grim-faced man spent his last hour with the priest
who administered the last rites.

Almost immediately after 11 A.M., the sheriff and deputies led Black to the gallows, where about forty persons gathered to witness the execution. They included the customary special deputies, physicians, and newspaper reporters as well as three of the jurors who convicted him. Black invited no family members or acquaintances, because "I have no friends who want to see me hang." As he walked firmly between the sheriff, on his right, and Father Cumminskey, someone placed a stiff, black hat upon his head as the trio went through the jail corridor.

Stepping outside into the raw, cold wind and flurries, Black calmly ascended the stairs of the scaffold. He paused before the trap door made white with snow even though attendants swept the platform half an hour earlier. The heavy flakes continued to fall on his hat as he bowed his pale face towards the floor. In his right hand he carried a gold cross that Father Cumminskey had given him earlier. The priest offered a brief, almost inaudible prayer before shaking hands for the last time with Black, who kissed the cross before returning it to the Catholic cleric.

With that last exchange, Black stepped upon the drop and stared directly through the noose as Deputy McKay firmly bound his arms and legs. After Sheriff Yund removed the hat to adjust the noose around the condemned man's neck, he asked, "George, have you anything to say?" "No," replied Black in a low voice, "I'm not the man that done the killing. That's all." With that, the sheriff slipped the dark hood over the convict's head before stepping aside to trip the trapdoor. At 11:13 A.M. Black dropped downward. For a full minute, the body did not move. Then the fingers twitched,

Sheriff Yund adjusts the noose around George Black's neck, on February 26, 1890. (Photo Courtesy American Heritage Center, University of Wyoming. *Copyright Restricted.*)

followed by a slight contraction of the legs. County Physician J.H. Finfrock and Doctor Stevens immediately joined Doctor Rickets of Carbon County to test Black's erratically failing pulse. Finally several minutes after the criminal fell through the trapdoor, the doctors tested his pulse. At thirty-second increments it was measured respectively at 50...54...36...38...34...32...24. Finally, at the end of twenty minutes, they pronounced death before assistants cut down the body and turned it over to the undertaker.

Before 1 P.M., Black's body found peace in the local Potter's Field, where he was buried at his request next to George Cooke, the only other man to be legally executed in Albany County.

POSTSCRIPT

By strange coincidence Sarah Black became ill with pneumonia the same day her estranged husband George was hanged. Failing rapidly, she died only nine days later on Friday, March 7.

And four days after that, Judge Saufley dismissed the indictment against Rockwell as an accessory after the crime and released him from jail. Not all agreed with the judge's decision, but the local press applauded Rockwell's release, because they believed he:

...could not have been convicted of even the offense for which he was indicted, by any evidence which has yet been discovered. We have seen and heard more of the history of this case than any other one, except Judge Groesbeck, and we fully believe that Rockwell told the truth, and the whole truth, in relation to it.

Free at last, Sheriff Yund and Bailiff Alky escorted the young man to the depot. He still had about twenty-five dollars which he had earned in North Park before his arrest, and he used that money to purchase a ticket aboard a train leaving that same evening for the west coast. Although Rockwell said he planned to return to the sea, he obviously made another wrong turn. A drunk shot and killed him in Montana just two years later.

Sources Sited

In addition to the primary source documents found in Albany County Second Judicial District Court Criminal Case File #464 and Wyoming Territorial Supreme Court Docket #2-76, additional colorful details were culled from a variety of newspapers including the *Boomerang* and *Laramie Weekly Sentinel* (Laramie, Wyoming) plus the *Cheyenne Daily Leader* (Cheyenne, Wyoming).

Specifics concerning the physical descriptions of the Black brothers is found in the *Register of Prisoners Convicted in County*, Albany County, Laramie, Wyoming, which is on file at the Wyoming State Archives.

Epilogue

AND SO, MORE THAN a century after Wyoming's justice system carried out its first legal execution, a total of twenty-six men have been punished—permanently—and their lives taken in return for the ones they stole from innocent men, women, and children. Twenty murderers hanged, seven of them while Wyoming was a territory. Five met their fate in the gas chamber. The last (at this writing in 1997), Mark Hopkinson, suffered an injection of deadly chemicals after having been found guilty of arranging, from his jail cell, the murder of a witness who prepared to testify against him.

For those great transgressions against God and man, fate chased those guilty wretches to the end of a dark path. There, each met the lady of law and found "...beneath her hood the inexorable face of death."

Appendix

John Boyer

Crime: Shot and killed William H. Lowry and James Mc-Clusky "for raping his mother and sister"

Location: At the Six Mile Hog Ranch saloon near Fort Laramie (then Laramie County)

Date/Time: 26 October 1870/shortly after midnight

Convicted: 23 March 1871, in Cheyenne (Laramie County seat)

Executed: 21 April 1871 at approximately 12:30 P.M. in Cheyenne in "an old grout building nearly in front of the jail on 16th St."

William "Tousant" Kensler

Crime: Shot and killed Adolph Peña, sheepherder, during a drunken argument over their prostitute sweetheart

Location: In the Six Mile Hog Ranch saloon near Ft. Laramie

Date/Time: 9 April 1872/evening

Convicted: December 1872, in Cheyenne

Executed: 19 November 1874 at 12:30 P.M. in Cheyenne in the McDonald Building at Bent and 21st Street near what was known as "Tracy's Corral"

JOHN LEROY DONOVAN
(AKA JOHN OR JACK LEE)

Crime: Bludgeoned to death William Leighton for the barber's savings

Location: Leighton's bedroom in Rock Springs (Sweetwater County)

Date/Time: 6 May 1883/very early morning

Convicted: 23 October 1884, in Rawlins (Carbon County seat)

Executed: 18 January 1884 at 11:45 A.M. in Rawlins in a corner where the east side of the Carbon County Jail adjoined the Carbon County Courthouse

GEORGE COOKE

Crime: Shot and killed his brother-in-law James Blount during a drunken argument

Location: In front of L. Rudolph Abram's saloon which was the second door down from J. Fred Hesse's saloon at 117 Front Street in Laramie

Date/Time: 28 November 1883 (Thanksgiving)/evening

Convicted: 7 December 1883 in Laramie (Albany County)

Executed: 12 December 1884 at 11:26 A.M. in Laramie within a two-story pine-slab shed some twenty feet square made expressly for that purpose outside the Albany County Courthouse

JOHN OWENS (AKA BILL BOOTH)

Crime: Beat Jacob Schmerer to death with a hatchet during a premeditated murder for the old German's money

Location: Inside Schmerer's cabin on Dry Creek, about six miles southeast of Buffalo

Date/Time: 25 March 1884/evening

Convicted: 10 July 1885 in Buffalo (Johnson County seat)

Executed: 5 March 1886 at 9:30 A.M. in Buffalo within the jail yard behind the Johnson County Courthouse

BENJAMIN F. CARTER

Crime: Shot and killed James Jeffries, young wrangler, during a cattle roundup

Location: Inside their sleeping tent about 30 miles northeast of Rawlins and six miles from Ferris near the Shirley Ranch

Date/Time: 4 October 1886/evening

Convicted: 21 May 1887 in Rawlins

Executed: 26 October 1888 at 10:37 A.M. on a gallows near the east wall of the Carbon County Courthouse yard.

GEORGE A. BLACK

Crime: Shot and killed Robert "Ol' Tanglefoot" Burnett

Location: Inside the old hermit's cabin on Pole Creek about fifteen miles northeast of Laramie

Date/Time: 28 May 1889/afternoon

Convicted: 16 November 1889 in Laramie (Albany County)

Executed: 26 February 1890 at 11:30 A.M. in Laramie on a scaffold within the same two-story wooden shed that was used for George Cooke's execution

INDEX

photo by
Craig Pindell

ABOUT THE AUTHOR

Larry K. Brown, a fifth generation published writer, earned a degree in Journalism from the University of Nebraska in 1960 before entering the U.S. Air Force where he spent the next twenty years as an Information/Public Affairs officer. During his military career, he graduated from Boston University with a Master of Science degree in Public Relations and Mass Communications.

In 1980 he went to work for the Sun Company, Inc. and five years later was named Director, Public Relations and Communications for Sun Exploration and Production Company. In 1987, Brown joined the staff of the American Heart Association (AHA) national headquarters, and the following year was sent to Wyoming, as the Executive Director, AHA-Wyoming, Inc.

His writing credits include more than 800 articles in such publications as *Wild West, True West, American Cowboy, Wyoming Magazine, Wyoming Annals,* and *Wyoming History Journal.* He also researched and scripted a two-hour *Today* show aired in 1979 by NBC-TV as well as a one-hour *Prime Time Sunday* program broadcast the following year by ABC-TV.

His *Hog Ranches of Wyoming: Liquor, Lust, and Lies Under Sagebrush Skies,* for which he received the "Western Horizon Award" from Wyoming Writers, Inc., was published in 1995 by High Plains Press. This is the second book of his Wyoming History Triology. The final book—*The Petticoat Prisoners of Old Wyoming*—is forthcoming from High Plains Press.

Brown is an Active Member of Western Writers of America and Wyoming Writers, Inc. He and wife Florence, who make their home in Cheyenne, have four grown children.

The text is composed in
twelve point Adobe Garamond.
Display type is Post Antiqua BE and Texas Hero.
The book is printed on
sixty-pound Gladtfelter Supple Opaque
acid-free, recycled paper
by Thomson-Shore.